Blue Remembered Hills

A memoir of childhood on the Welsh borders

Eleanor Watkins

O&U

Onwards & Upwards

Onwards and Upwards Publishers

4 The Old Smithy
London Road
Rockbeare
Exeter
EX5 2EA
United Kingdom
www.onwardsandupwards.org

First edition, published in the United Kingdom by Onwards and Upwards Publishers Ltd. (2019).

ISBN: 978-1-78815-626-4
Typeface: Sabon LT
Graphic design: LM Graphic Design

Author's note:

Some names and identifying details have been changed to protect the privacy of individuals.

About the Author

 Eleanor Watkins was born on a remote hill farm and has lived in a rural community all her life. As soon as she could read, she knew she wanted to write stories too. Her first paid piece of writing was at the age of twenty-one, her first book ten years later. Over the years, forty-four books have followed, most of them fiction for children and young adults, plus numerous short stories and articles. The most recent are the *Beech Bank Girls* series with Dernier Publishing and *The Village* series with Books to Treasure, with more in the pipeline. Eleanor loves the countryside, gardening, travel, reading. She lives with her husband in an old farmhouse overlooking the beautiful Wye Valley near the book town of Hay-on-Wye, and they have four adult children and five grand-children.

To my brother Ron,
my best friend in childhood
and partner in crime;

and to our little brother Tim;

and all of our children, grandchildren
and the great-grandchild who is
the first of a new generation;

and to all who will come after them.

And to the memory of our parents,
Baden and Gretta.

'What are those blue remembered hills
What spires, what farms are those?

This is the land of lost content
I see it shining plain,
The happy highways where I went
And cannot come again.'

- A.E. Housman -
From 'A Shropshire Lad'

Contents

Blue Remembered Hills

Foreword by Oliver Balch

Childhood memories are strange and rather wonderful things. In part, this is because, as adults, we too quickly forget how vast and voracious, how beautiful and beguiling, is the world around us. But as children, our surroundings have the capacity to constantly entrance and amaze. We are primed for puzzlement, prepped for surprise. Thus the nature of the childhood memoir is without exception an act of historical reconstruction. It invites the author to re-enter the universe of childhood and re-tread its winding paths. Old experiences must be mined, old memories dusted down. It is no easy task, this resuscitation of the past, not only because our recollections cloud with time, but because the book's author and lead actor have diverged. The protagonist of the childhood memoir is the writer, and yet not the writer. Time has placed a distance between the two. It is hard to fathom, being one and yet not one, but so it is.

Neither of these obstacles seem to trouble Eleanor. In this charming and deeply touching memoir, she draws on her long experience of storytelling to vividly bring to life her upbringing in the hills of the Welsh borders. As with all the best writers, she totally immerses herself in her story's internal world. There is no 'back then' and 'now'. When she writes, she is there in person, present and wide-eyed, watching her mother turn the handle of the butter churn, or observing her father harnessing up his work horse. The fear she feels as she sits waiting for the school dentist (reckoned also to be a butcher) is visceral and true. So too is the joy and freedom she feels climbing trees with her brother Ron, and scratching her knees as she scrambles through hedgerows. She succeeds in bridging the decades, inhabiting the rural world of yesteryear as though it were today. It is an uncanny skill, gained, I suspect, for never letting the child in her die. Her writing rings loud with childlike wonderment. It is this gift that for years has made her children's books sparkle. Now, to the reader's delight, she has turned her pen to her own story. The result is a tale as enchanting as any fable, and as heart-warming as any romance.

There is much in *Blue Remembered Hills* that reminds me of *Kilvert's Diary*, which covers an identical geography but is set some seven decades earlier. Eleanor shares the same love for people and place as the diarist, a young Victorian curate, Francis Kilvert. There is much Kilvert would have recognised about her childhood world, living as she did in a 'primitive' farmhouse with no electricity or hot water supply, six people in three bedrooms, and an hour's walk from the village. As in Kilvert's day, everyone knew everyone else by name: Dr Crawford, the kindly, bespectacled school doctor; Mrs Williams, the unofficial midwife, nurse and 'layer-out' of the dead; Mrs Layton Lwyn Gwilliam with her four pretty daughters; the Reverend Lloyd, a gentle, silver-haired saint. Even the fields had names: Wernypentre Field; Tynessa meadows. But, as keen an observer as he was, Kilvert was always that: the outsider looking in. Eleanor, in contrast, was as embedded in local life as it is possible to be. Nothing in this rich and personal account comes second-hand. Everything she describes – changing seasons, farm life, playground games, details of the food and fashions of the day – all are lived and breathed and recorded for posterity.

Life was not always easy growing up in a rural corner of Wales in the wake of World War II. Money was tight and daily foodstuffs were still rationed. Yet *Blue Remembered Hills* is full of joy and contentment, a testament to the value of a loving family and a secure home. It is difficult to discern much of Eleanor's childhood world today. The days of the 'wireless' and Syrup of Figs are long gone. No-one today would suck on cloves to ease toothache or read in bed by candlelight. In this respect, *Blue Remembered Hills* earns its place as an exemplary social history of rural life in mid-20th century Wales. But it is so much more than that as well. Told in clear and natural prose, it is a paean to the simple things in life. It reminds us of what a 'good' childhood really is, regardless of age or epoch. Above all else, children need to know they are loved. That way, like Eleanor, they can love in return – love family and friends, love schoolmates and neighbours, but above all, love life itself. Here, *Blue Remembered Hills* truly excels. It is a book that not only informs and entertains, but one that warms the soul.

Oliver Balch is a freelance journalist and travelogue author. His books include Viva South America, India Rising and Under the Tump: Sketches of real life in the Welsh borders.

Introduction

A certain drama surrounded the event of my birth. It was wartime, the country was in the grip of a hard winter, my family were snowbound, and my parents were virtually homeless.

I was born in a lonely farmhouse, hunched against the winter with its back to the Begwyns, on a January day when the farm was deep in snowdrifts. My parents had been obliged to leave the farm they had been occupying, their next home was not ready, and they had been taken in by my mother's sister, Auntie Mary, her husband, Uncle Idris, and their two young daughters. A midwife was needed, deep drifts covered the roadways, and my father, uncle and a gang of neighbours with shovels had to clear a way for her to come. The birth was not straightforward or speedy; the midwife had to stay for a night and possibly more, sharing a bed with my mother. This was not unusual; midwives sometimes did stay over, taking care of mother and baby and often looking after other children in the family and doing household chores as well. So everyone waited, while elsewhere the war raged, snow fell, and the work of the farm went on, until at last I arrived, the first child of my parents, on a chilly Saturday morning, alive and well and weighing a healthy eight and a half pounds.

My childhood home on Clyro Court estate

CHAPTER ONE

A World at War

The happiest people do not have the best of everything. They make the best of everything they have.

Unknown

Great Britain (as it was still called) had been at war with Germany for sixteen months by the time the first day of January, 1941, dawned cold, wintry and subdued. Formerly the leaders and conquerors of a vast and powerful empire that covered half the globe, a devastating and horrific war that wiped out a whole generation of young men and changed the face of history had changed Britain too, almost beyond recognition, barely more than twenty years before. Britain, bailed out by the United States of America and still reeling from the effects of the Great War, had nevertheless pulled itself together and, first voiced by author H.G. Wells, had declared that World War 1 must be the 'war to end all wars'. Politician David Lloyd George had more cynically commented that 'this war, like the next war, is a war to end war'. Nevertheless, the League of Nations had been formed, an international body set up to regulate the world, outlaw war and protect the rights of small nations. Armaments were to be reduced worldwide. A Peace Conference taking place in 1919 held great hopes for the future. The British Empire, though still large in territory, could no longer be maintained and defended; the War Debt of £900 million owed to the United States had to be repaid, and there was no longer money for building military bases and ships. But Britain would rise again. With the threat of war now in the past, a better world would emerge. Wouldn't it?

Any such hopes were dashed in September 1939 with a sombre announcement from the Prime Minister and a swift plunge into another war that would again engulf the world and wipe out 55 million people.

By 1941, momentous events were unfolding. France and Belgium had fallen to the German forces. In the previous May and June, 350,000 French, Belgian and British troops, driven to the coast by the advancing

German army and trapped on the beaches of Dunkirk, had been rescued in dramatic and heroic circumstances, many saved by the flotilla of fishing boats, pleasure craft and other 'little ships' who courageously crossed the channel to join in the rescue. The Blitz had begun in September 1940, with London bombed by the Luftwaffe for fifty-seven consecutive nights. More than a million London homes had been destroyed and more than 40,000 civilians killed. In 1941, the bombing would extend to the port towns of Liverpool, Hull, Bristol, Cardiff, Portsmouth, Plymouth, Southampton and Swansea, as well as the industrial cities of Birmingham, Belfast, Coventry, Manchester, Glasgow and Sheffield. Coventry Cathedral had been destroyed. Llandaff Cathedral in Cardiff had been bombed. All through the summer of 1940 the Battle of Britain had raged in the skies, and in September Hitler recognised the futility of the proposed German invasion, Operation Sea Lion, and the plan was abandoned. There were rousing speeches by Churchill. The country girded its loins for whatever might happen next.

In other parts of the world, offensives and counter-offensives were happening, in Albania, Libya, Italy, Eritrea and Sudan. The persecution of Jews had begun in European countries. The United States had not yet entered the war arena, but already there were muted warnings and rumours of a possible attack on Pearl Harbour.

Back home, with merchant shipping unable to deliver, rationing of food had come into being, beginning with butter, cheese and sugar. Gas masks had been issued to the population, with the fear of an attack of the deadliest of all, mustard gas, and had to be carried at all times in a brown cardboard box. Fines were imposed on anyone found without their gas mask. Children from the big cities were evacuated to the country.

The country. Here, surely, in a sleepy village or a farm tucked into the fold of sheltering hills, the children of the towns and cities would be safe. And they were, on the whole, though some were more fortunate than others in their placements and the way they were treated by their host families. Most would return to their own families, but there were those who stayed when the war ended and made their lives and their futures in the countryside. I know someone who was bombed out of Coventry as a tiny baby and taken in by a farm couple. She never re-bonded with her own family, but stayed for good with her 'auntie' and 'uncle', married and brought up her own children in the lush Hereford countryside and lives to this day in a small rural village. There were many like her.

I was still a small child when the war ended, but I have some memories of that time. I remember the ugly khaki-coloured gas masks with their goggle eyes and protruding respirators. I had a child's Mickey Mouse mask, a colourful affair that was a little less scary than the adult ones. My baby brother had a kind of protective container that the baby was put into wholesale. I don't remember ever wearing the masks. The expected mustard gas attacks never happened. I don't think we ever toted the things around with us either.

We weren't required to have evacuees; goodness knows there were enough of us sharing a three-bedroomed house as it was, with my grandmother and aunt living there as well. I have vague impressions of meeting other children now and then at neighbours' houses, bigger children than me, who talked in a strange way. I think we had land girls for a time, shapely creatures in brown dungarees, who smoked and laughed and talked loudly (again with accents strange to us) and unlike ourselves, were not at all shy. I imagine they were based at another farm and hired out to help at busy times.

And there were prisoners of war, a gang guarded by a man with a gun who supervised them as they dug drainage trenches on a boggy eleven-acre field of ours. We must have watched them working at some point; I have mental images of men with picks and shovels working in the mud, wearing mud-coloured clothes. There was a fresh-faced, fair-haired young man, obviously a 'trusty', who came to the farmhouse every day to fetch milk. He took notice of us children and told us in his broken English that he had a little boy of his own at home. I hope they were re-united after the war and had happy lives. Maybe the little boy is still alive and well and has children and grandchildren.

And there were the planes. Planes were in the skies, sometimes whole flotillas. The grown-ups would fall silent as they watched the planes fly over. I didn't understand, had no knowledge of warfare in the skies, but from the hushed way they talked I knew that things were happening, things to do with planes and that they were bad things. Later I learned that planes dropped bombs, and every time one droned into earshot I was terrified it would drop a bomb on us. I remember the profound relief I felt as the droning sound faded away into the distance. We had escaped once again! I would dream of them at night, planes dropping bombs and planes crashing in flames. The fear of planes lasted well into adult life, and I still have the occasional nightmare about a plane coming down and crashing nearby, a dream so vivid that I think, still dreaming, *there, it was real all the time!*

CHAPTER TWO

The Francis Family

Call it a clan, call it a network, call it a tribe, call it a family;
whatever you call it, you need one.

Jane Howard

*M*emory is a strange thing and can play tricks. No two people's memories of the same event will be quite the same. Sometimes, incidents or family stories, repeated often enough, become embedded in the mind and recorded as a memory of one's own.

I think I remember the birth of my brother Ron when I was no more than a toddler myself. My mother always said there was an eighteen-month gap between us in age, but in fact I was nineteen months and a week when he arrived. I have a memory of sitting in a little chair, squeezed between two large pieces of furniture in our kitchen. One of these, I think, was a wooden chest of drawers painted pale green. The paint was chipped in places. There were a great many doors in our kitchen, five in all, opening into the back kitchen, the pantry, the hall, the cupboard under the stairs and one that led to the staircase itself, plain wooden steps with a dog-leg twist on the way up. That particular August day, the stairs door opened and my aunt came through with a shawl-wrapped bundle in her arms. My baby brother was here! I don't remember whether this was a big surprise, or how he looked, what I felt, whether I loved him or was jealous or anything else. I have no recall of him laughing or crying or sitting up or learning to walk. My mother told me that when she breast-fed him, I would sit beside her and stuff my toy squirrel up my jumper. I have no memory of that either, although I remember the squirrel, pale yellow and hand-knitted in garter-stitch.

By this time we had been living on our own rented farm since the spring of the year before, moving when I was three months old. A great deal of turbulence and at least one family rift had preceded the move. My father was already in his late thirties when he married, my mother eleven years younger. I have no idea where they met, what the circumstances were, how long they knew each other. The wedding was a simple one, no big family gathering, no wedding breakfast that I know of, just a simple ceremony with a few family members. It was wartime, frugality was the keyword. It was a freezing cold February day; icicles hung from the branches of the trees outside the church. My father wore a 3-piece suit with a carnation in his buttonhole and looked elegant; he was 6'3" tall and lean with it, formal suits looked good on him. My mother wore a navy suit (called a 'costume' in those days) and a wide-brimmed navy hat. She had navy kid gloves and navy court shoes but no bouquet of flowers; strange, as flowers and growing things were one of her great lifelong passions. But I suppose nothing would be in bloom in the gardens, and the expense of buying cut flowers, even if they were available, would be out of the question. There are few pictures of the day. The honeymoon was spent in Hereford and, I imagine, was brief, probably no more than a weekend.

Their search for the tenancy of a farm of their own had been beset by pitfalls. My father was the eldest son of my grandparents, born as a new century began, in 1900. My Grandad Francis was something of a character. From a farming background, he nevertheless had a nomadic streak and moved about a great deal. All of his five children were born in different parts of England and Wales, wherever they happened to be at the time. After my dad, Pryce Baden, always known as Baden, came William (Uncle Will), Arthur, Archie and finally, when my father was sixteen or seventeen, a daughter, Rose. Rose, who died in 2007 at the age of ninety-one, recalled that when her dad got the urge to move on, he upped and went, no discussion, no arguments, no consideration of preferences, or schools, or any other obstacle that might get in the way. He worked as a gamekeeper as well as a farmer, employed by local gentry who owned vast estates in those days. When Baden was ten, the family migrated to Canada where they tried farming in Ontario. It didn't work out, they returned to Britain a year later. I believe the extremes of cold and heat affected my grandmother's health very badly. My dad remembered being in school there for a while and that the winter was bitterly cold. I have one of his little cloth-covered school readers from that time, the Ontario First Reader.

My grandfather, I would imagine, ruled his family with a rod of iron. My grandmother, at some point, had sustained an accident that left her crippled and bent double; I vaguely remember being told that she had slipped on ice. She walked bowed over, shuffling and using a crutch, but managing the affairs of the household none the less. She had white hair pulled back into a tight bun, and if she had been able to stand straight, would have been a tall, slender women like her daughter Rose. She must have endured pain, but I never heard her complain, in fact a dry, wry sense of humour sometimes showed itself. She never questioned her husband's authority, and as far as I know, seldom if ever left her house, dairy and garden, where she worked as hard as any other farmer's wife.

My father, the eldest, had probably been marked down from the start as the one who would work the farm with his father. Possibly to escape these constraints, or maybe because of the intense patriotic fever that gripped the country at the time, my father signed up to the army as a teenage volunteer, as did many others at the outset of World War 1. His age, posting and length of service are somewhat cloaked in mystery, but he was only eighteen in the year the war ended so must have been considerably underage, but he was a tall lad and the recruiting powers-that-be often winked an eye. He was a musician and we learned later that he had played the *Last Post* on the cornet at countless funerals for comrades who had died of the flu that swept the world at that time. I do not think he ever left the country to serve in France. Nevertheless the war left its mark on him, as it did on everyone who served and survived. Throughout his life my father suffered bouts of deep depression, when he would withdraw from his family and from everyday life. My childhood was unclouded by these changes of mood and I only became aware of them in my teen years; probably because of my mother, who believed in shielding her children from the harsher realities of life. There is further mystery about his discharge, although family opinion has it that Grandad Francis somehow intervened and yanked him out to return to the family farm, wherever it happened to be at that time. He dutifully stayed for another twenty years. His brother next in age, Will, escaped quite soon and emigrated to Canada where he became a hunter, trapper and game-warden before returning to Great Britain, marrying and settling down. He and his wife Daisy had a daughter, my cousin Betty, three years older than me, whom I did not get to meet until we were both mothers of teenage boys. The third son, Arthur, or Art, died tragically young after a kick to his head by a horse, which left him brain-damaged and epileptic. Rose, the daughter, tall, dark-haired, slim and attractive – and very strictly under her father's thumb – made her escape by eloping with a German prisoner-of-war employed on the farm. The outrage and scandal can be imagined; for a while Rose and her alien husband were disowned by her family. Her husband, Ludwig (or Uncle Lou as we knew him), proved to be a devoted husband and father to their two daughters. They settled in Birmingham and were happily married for more than fifty years. Archie, the youngest son, a gentle, kindly, peaceable man, never married and stayed with his parents to the ends of their lives.

My parents were interested in taking the tenancy of a fertile, red-soiled farm belonging to Whitbourne Hall in the depths of rural Herefordshire. My father had been to view it, maybe my mother too, and wanted his father's opinion of the property. A visit was arranged, the shameful outcome of which I only heard when I was well into middle-age. My dad no doubt valued his father's opinions and hoped that the place would find favour in his eyes. It was, after all, a place with huge possibilities, a rich, fertile piece of the shire, in the heart of cider-growing and Hereford cattle breeding country, with a magnificent farmhouse of mellow red brick in an idyllic setting. His father did approve, so much so that he took a strong fancy to it himself, decided that another move was desirable, applied for and got the tenancy for himself, cruelly leaving my parents high and dry. They had been living in another of his properties which was sold, leaving my parents virtually homeless at the time I was born.

So it was that we found ourselves instead on a hundred and eighteen acres of border hill country, some of it in need of drainage, with woodland and a stream, on land belonging to the Clyro Court estate, home of the Baskerville family, in a stone built farmhouse that lacked even the basic amenities but had the most wonderful view of the Black Mountains and the beautiful Wye valley.

CHAPTER THREE

The Stephens Family

You don't choose your family. They are God's gift to you, as you are to them.

Desmond Tutu

From our front door, you stepped out on to a raised area the length of the house. Today it might be called a patio, then it was simply known as 'the front'. There were stone slabs and steps leading down to the farmyard. On either side, flower beds; a jasmine bush; a very pretty orange-red flowered shrub, called, I think, *Chaenomeles japonica Sargentii;* a clematis with huge purple-blue flowers that scrambled round the front door; a yew tree at the end on the left. Traditionally planted in churchyards, yew trees were also often found beside a farmhouse, symbols of regeneration and eternity, all parts of it highly toxic but possessing amazing abilities to spring back to life even after severe pruning. A narrow stone-flag path ran along the outer edge of the front, all surrounded by a wooden picket-fence. A gate fastened across the bottom of the steps, presumably to keep livestock out and maybe small children in, although I remember it as always being open.

From the front, the Black Mountains loomed on the horizon, their shapes as familiar as our own kitchen and the faces of our family. I puzzled over why they were called the Black Mountains, as they were always blue, a slatey purple-blue hazed by distance, with here and there the white dot of a farmhouse on the lower slopes. We lived at an altitude of 900 feet; those mountains were even higher, Hay Bluff soaring to 2,200 feet, Lord Hereford's Knob, or the Twmpa, higher still at 2,600 feet and often with its head in the clouds. Between them, the Gospel Pass cut through on its way from Hay-on-Wye to Llanthony Abbey and on to Abergavenny. As children we knew nothing of those names. The mountains were just there, immovable and unchanging, although they seemed much nearer if rain was threatening, and more remote and far away when the weather was fine. Below them, the open mountainside merged and softened into farmland that straggled downhill to the valley and the silver ribbon of the Wye running through. Even now, when travelling and marvelling at some magnificent range of mountains, in North Wales or Shropshire, or Ireland or Scotland or California, their shape seems to jar a little. They are not the familiar mountains imprinted on my mind since childhood.

The view was spectacular, but the conditions of our house could only be described as basic, or even primitive, though it all seemed normal to us. We were also somewhat overcrowded, six people sharing three bedrooms because my maternal grandmother and my aunt also lived with us. I never questioned why they were there, just accepted that they were, and I loved them both. I know they enriched our lives. Piecing things together in later life, I realised that my grandmother's place on her family farm had been usurped by her daughter-in-law, the wife of her second son Tom, who had taken over the farm. My Auntie Lizzie, her eldest and unmarried daughter still living at home, must also have been in the way; more than one woman sharing a kitchen is not a recipe for harmony. Having said that, three women did just that in our home for several years without any friction that I remember. The fact that the other two were my mum's mother and her sister, and that the three of them were very close, must have helped. My dad must have felt somewhat outnumbered by females, though I never saw any trace of resentment.

My Granny Stephens' life had known real tragedy. She had been one of a very large family, the Ammonds, some of them farming people but not all; a surprising variety of occupations and lifestyles comes to light when their history is delved into a little. One branch of the family migrated to Yorkshire and kept a butcher's shop. Another, I believe, or maybe the same one at a different time, kept the Angel Inn in Loftus, North Yorkshire. Strangely, my younger brother, researching for his own memoir on his experiences in Iran, discovered that a work colleague[1] remembered that a descendant of the Ammonds family, Dickie Nutt, son of the station master at Withernsea, had once lodged at his family home. Dickie appears to have been the 'black sheep' of his family and had been kicked out of his own family home! Small world.

---

[1] My brother and his work colleague were two of the handful of Europeans left in Iran after the 1978 revolution. See *Shadows Over Iran* by Tim Francis, published by lulu.com

One of my grandmother's nephews, Tom Ammonds, became an expert on wildlife and birds, eccentric but well respected. His sister Jessie was a missionary with the China Inland Mission for many years, only leaving when forced out in the 1940s. I met her a couple of times, the first time as a child at the home of a mutual relative when Jessie was home on furlough. I half-expected to see a frumpy severe person in long skirts, but met instead a rather striking, slim, dark-haired lady in a smart green tweed suit, with a sheepskin waistcoat over it because she felt the British cold so terribly. She was vivacious and lively and fascinating. I have some of her early exploits, written in tiny cramped writing on little squares of thin paper, sent home in wartime. She ministered mostly to groups of women, travelling alone the length and breadth of her area on an ancient bicycle which often broke down. An excerpt from one of her early letters home reads:

> ...a little further along, I besought the aid of a bikeshaw man. The air wouldn't go in[to the tyre] and we found on investigation that the valve rubber was rotted ... after some badgering of the gentleman he sold me a new one and fixed it and away went I ... about 6 miles further along was pedal trouble, I found my left pedal all hanging loose ... I tied that up with a string torn from my straw hat and away again went we. The last ten miles the stupid old thing clucked all the way – I investigated to no avail so rode on regardless and clucking ... it was the funniest of journeys ... My first journey in China all alone, yet certainly not alone, how the Lord undertook, I just praise Him.

How gratified she would be to know that her work was not in vain, that, far from being stamped out under persecution, Christianity in China is probably the fastest growing and most vibrant and flourishing faith group in today's world.

Another of my mother's cousins, Tom Nutt, was the pharmacist in Hay-on-Wye for many years. He lived in a large house called Humberstone on the edge of town, and invited us children to visit and watch special events, like the *Trooping of the Colour*, on his television set. TV was a huge novelty to us in our childhood. On one occasion his grown-up daughter Jeanne was home from London on a visit. She wore elegant grey linen slacks and was making a summer dress of some gauzy flowered material. She served us lemonade and biscuits, and was very kind to a pair of shy country kids, asking about our school and interests. What we didn't know at the time was that Jeanne actually worked for the diplomatic service and was a personal secretary to the Prime Minister of the time, Sir Anthony Eden, eventually marrying the British Ambassador to Moscow, Sir Iain Sutherland, and becoming closely involved with the diplomatic service in embassies from Russia to Cuba and Greece.

Some of my grandmother's cousins emigrated to the United States, settling on farms in Texas and Idaho. One of them, Evan Worthing, first worked on the developing railroad, then went into property development. Through contact with some of his African American tenants, he became concerned at the lack of opportunity for their young people. Evan became a millionaire, remained unmarried and childless, and on his death, bequeathed most of his fortune to setting up establishments for the education of young African Americans. The Evan E. Worthing schools and colleges he founded remain and flourish to this day. As one of my nephews remarked, 'He was one of the good guys.'

Others in the family became doctors, nurses and teachers. One of my grandmother's sisters married a vicar, who also had the added distinction of having written a book! I was very impressed by that, but when I finally read the book, I found it rather disappointingly dull. My great-grandmother had been a Honeyfield, a name which appears here and there among the Christian names of her descendants. My grandmother was Eleanor Honeyfield. I am named after her and my youngest granddaughter is named after me. I am rather sorry now that the Honeyfield bit has been dropped in recent generations; it has a certain evocative ring to it though I found it odd as a child. My grandmother was known as Nellie, or Nell.

Nell was married in 1898, to a young man called James Stephens. She was twenty-eight and he was thirty-three. It seems to have been regarded as a perfect match, the young couple set up for a busy, happy future. A letter from a cousin who had settled in Switzerland reads:

> *...Just a line to wish you all happiness in your new life. I think it must be a happy one for you as our new homes and new lives are very much what we make them ourselves. ... Good daughters make good wives, good wives make good husbands and good husbands make happy homes, with God's blessing come prosperity and increase, what more can any mortal ask*

for ... I enclose a cheque to help you get the butter-worker
your brother said you'd like. Do not get too big a one, it is
much better I find to work up the butter twice when there is
20 lb of it than to do it all at once...

I believe she made her wedding dress. I've seen pictures of my grandmother as a child but none of her as a wife and mother. Probably she was too busy for photographs. She and Jim set up farming at Tyllemawr, Glasbury-on-Wye, which is still in the Stephens family. I know little of my grandfather, except that he was a good farmer, well respected, a parish councillor. Within a space of fifteen years, Jim and Nell had a growing family of seven children: James, Elizabeth, Mary, Edith, Thomas, Frederick and Emily Margaretta, my mother. Unusually at that time, there do not appear to have been any infant fatalities, or none that were recorded. The farm prospered. The oldest son, known as Jimmie, won a scholarship to Grammar School, a rare opportunity in those days when the school-leaving age was fourteen. Tragedy struck in late December of 1913, when my grandfather contracted meningitis and died within a few days. There was nothing that could be done. Swift treatment with antibiotics might have saved him, but antibiotics were still many decades in the future. He was forty-eight.

The tributes poured in and the neighbours turned out in full strength for the funeral. Not just farmers, but auctioneers, councillors, tradesmen, business people. My grandfather had been well loved and respected. My mother remembered, as a toddler of two and a half, standing with her boy cousin of the same age and watching the funeral procession from behind the farm gate. She had no other memory of her father.

With seven children to raise and a farm to run, my grandmother must have been sorely pressed. But Jim's brother David had already been living with the family and helping to run the farm, so he did much to fill the breach with the farm work and act as male role model to the fatherless children. They remembered him with affection, but he could be a stern surrogate parent. For some reason, my mother was always 'Julie' to him. She told a story of being collared by Uncle Davey and severely reprimanded for jumping on a newly planted patch of vegetable garden. I can't remember what the punishment was, but she took it without complaint. 'And it wasn't even me that did it,' she told me with a touch of indignation, decades later. 'It was Tom and Fred!'

'Didn't you tell him it wasn't you?' I asked.

'No,' she said, 'you didn't answer back to Uncle Davey. If he said something was so, then it was so.'

Jimmie, the eldest, had to forego his further education and stay home to work on the farm. He took on something of a parental role as well. By the end of the next year the country was at war, and my mother remembered being told by Jimmie, if anyone fussed about food, that they must eat everything on their plates 'because there are boys in the trenches who are not getting enough to eat'. My mother and most of her generation took this to heart; waste of food was a cardinal sin and all her life she found it impossible to throw away anything.

None of my grandmother's sons were eligible to go to war, but when it was all over in 1919, another tragedy overtook the family. Edie, the third daughter, was epileptic and subject to fits. She was an exceptionally bright and intelligent child; some held the opinion that her 'brain had developed too fast for her body'. Her family had hoped that she would outgrow the fits. But it was not to be. When she was thirteen, she had a fit while she was getting dressed alone in her bedroom and strangled with the string fastenings of one of her garments. My mother and aunt used to tell me, with a touch of tragic drama, that she had been buried a day before her fourteenth birthday. I identified with Edie, who had won many competitions with her short stories for the local paper, and my lively imagination sometimes feared that I would share the same fate. When my fourteenth birthday came and went without incident, I breathed a sigh of relief.

CHAPTER FOUR

The House We Lived In

This old house once knew his children
This old house once knew his wife
This old house was home and comfort
As they fought the storms of life.

Stuart Hamblen

Our house was, I suppose, typical of many farmhouses dotted about the hills and valleys of mid-Wales; stone built, slate-roofed, perched on a slope. It faced south, and so caught all the sunshine that came; however, the builders, whoever they were, had had no notion of capturing light with large expanses of glass, which would have been extravagant, expensive and impractical on a hill farm. So all the windows were on the small side, casements opening outward, with the exception of a long, rather elegant window boasting a window seat in the best parlour and a skylight in the back kitchen. There was a front door with a handle and a back door with a latch. The back door was used more frequently that the front, but I remember the front door thrown open in the summer, and we children playing on the sun-warmed stone slabs outside.

The back door opened into the back kitchen, a chilly and unheated region with a stone sink and the one cold tap that supplied all our water needs. Beside it, under the tiny window, was a boiler with a small furnace, intended, I suppose, for washing clothes, though I think it was seldom used for that purpose, or the furnace lit. The boiler may have been used for storage purposes; there was a wooden cover over the top that was always cluttered with anything that needed dumping – animal drenches, garden stuff, small tools, my father's shaving mug (white pottery with a red rose decoration). My father shaved in the back kitchen, working up a good lather and scraping it off with a fearsome-looking razor, peering into the small mirror beside the back door. I don't think the shaving happened every day. He looked nice freshly shaved, but I remember him with bristly whiskers in between.

The back kitchen also housed other assorted items; a wooden dresser, a hand-operated galvanised washing machine, a high shelf of sinister dark bottles containing sheep drenches, liniments and other potions for the treatment of farm animals. There was a temperamental oil stove that my mother disliked and avoided cooking on whenever possible, preferring to use the kitchen range. There was also a pile of firewood in one corner, and a pig-bucket, repository for greasy washing-up water, scraps, vegetable peel and anything else edible to pigs.

At the end of the back kitchen a door led into the dairy, dim and cool, a small window at the far end covered in wire mesh to keep out insects in the summer, with wooden shutters for when it was cold. A sturdy stone slab ran the length of the room on one side, holding a meat safe, salted sides of bacon, bowls of cream, pats of butter and other perishables. No such things as fridges in those days, not in our house anyway. Various butter-making equipment stood along the other side, the cream separator, butter-worker and churn, along with sundry crocks and galvanised buckets. The milk, brought in twice a day fresh from the cow, went through a kind of production line, first put through a strainer to remove any particles of dust, dirt, insects or any other foreign body that might have fallen in during the milking process. Enough milk for the day would be dipped out and kept in jugs for our daily needs, whole milk with a good layer of cream on the top, no semi-skimmed, pasteurised or otherwise treated ever passed our lips. The remainder was then poured into the big galvanised bowl of the separator, and went through a series of pipes and floats, emerging as thick cream into a waiting crock on a swivel stand though one pipe, and skim milk for the pig into a bucket from the other. The separator was turned by hand, with a grinding sound and a ping at every turn, gathering speed as one progressed. When several days' worth of cream had accumulated, usually by the time it had soured, it was tipped into the churn. The barrel-shaped wooden churn was hand-worked too, the handle turning the churn end over end until the butter 'came', which was discernible by the subtle shift in the feel of it turning, a thump and a slosh instead of just a sloshing sound. There was also a little clear window where we could inspect the progress of the butter. The bung was removed, buttermilk ran into a bucket, the buttery curds were washed with water and then turned on to the butter-worker, squeezed with wooden rollers to extract the last moisture, salted, slapped about with wooden paddles called 'hands' and finally shaped into yellow pats, weighed, stamped and arranged on greaseproof paper to await market day. Butter-making equipment had to be scrupulously clean, the wooden parts scalded with boiling water before use, the separator with its myriad metal disks, pipes and cups taken apart, washed, scalded and put back together, a time-consuming task after each milking, twice a day.

Back through the door, a step down to the left and there was the kitchen, where the main living of the household went on. My mother had painted the walls a sunny yellow, maybe to compensate for the lack of light from the rather small window. It was a homely room, a solid square table in the middle easily seating eight, a glowing fire in the range. The range was already old-fashioned by the time I was at school; some of my friends had gleaming electric or gas cookers or Rayburns. Our range was a monster and subject to moods and sulks, the fire had to be kept burning brightly to heat the boiler on one side and the oven on the other. Even so, cakes and tarts had a way of coming out more cooked on one side than the other, to my mother's frustration. She had a tormented relationship with her cooking appliances and freely admitted that she disliked cooking, but still managed to turn out wonderful meals, cakes, pies, tarts and puddings. The kitchen floor was of large flagstones, softened by a rag rug in front of the fire. We worked the rugs ourselves, hooking strips of old clothing on to a hessian backing. The kitchen furniture was a hotchpotch, wooden cupboards and chests of drawers, a bulging bookcase, a sagging old sofa and armchair. A sturdy wooden table stood in the middle of the room, with room to seat eight on wooden kitchen chairs. An oil lamp lit the dark evenings. A bread oven was set in the wall at one side, my father's guns rested on a rack up among the ceiling beams. There was a little wall cupboard near the window where my mother kept, I think, medicines and remedies. There was a door to a cluttered cupboard under the stairs, a dim pantry with a big metal flour bin and rows of shelves holding jams, marmalades, pickles, bottled fruit, chutneys and packets of dry goods. My father's filing system, a bent wire on which he speared all his bills, invoices, receipts and various other documents, hung from the ceiling. At some point during my childhood he acquired a roll-top desk with intricate pigeonholes, which filled us with admiration. A radio (known then as the 'wireless') stood atop one of the cupboards, and behind it flowed an ever-increasing pile of newspapers, magazines and farming periodicals, growing higher and higher until they toppled over and collapsed in an untidy heap. It then fell to someone (often me) to rearrange, discard and create a tidy stack. A fireguard stood round the fire most of the time and there was a brass rod under the mantelpiece above, both of which were handy for the airing of laundry items. Out of sight behind the sofa languished a tangle of boots, wellies, slippers and other footwear, carelessly thrown there by their owners until someone took it upon themselves to arrange them neatly in pairs.

This, then, was our daily living space, the heart of the home. Through another door, across the front hall, and one entered a different world, the parlour, which had much more of an air of gentility. This was a large square room, with pale mushroom-coloured walls, a floor of dark polished wood, a gracious long window with a window seat. I wished the window seat could be used as such, with comfortable cushions, but it always housed a row of large prickly cacti in ornamental pots. There was a pretty fireplace and a fender with twin corner pieces of coal and wood boxes, their lids topped with a seat of polished leather. Brass candlesticks in graduated sizes stood along the mantelpiece. Flanking the fireplace were a pair of brown leather armchairs with brown velvet cushions and flat-topped arms of polished wood, very handy for resting one's cup of tea (with a saucer, of course – mugs were never used for hot beverages). There was no sofa in this room, but a pair of graceful wicker chairs which had their covers changed along with the seasons. In winter they wore a cosy chenille in warm shades of russet and cream; in summer they blossomed out in flowery chintz. In the middle of the room was the mandatory table and chairs, much smarter than the everyday ones, the table polished and gate-legged, the chairs upholstered. One of the pairs of chairs were genuine Heppelwhite; unfortunately, the seats had deteriorated and been replaced with flat plain board, which spoiled the effect when bare but were disguised with seat cushions. There were several other interesting pieces of furniture in the room, which I took for granted at the time but later came to realise were antiques of some value: a mahogany-coloured bow-fronted chest of drawers inlaid with marquetry, with brass handles and a high sheen; a glass-fronted cabinet stuffed to capacity with ornaments, china figures, knick-knacks and curios, some of them inherited from relatives who had travelled the world; a Bible box of some dark carved wood, complete with huge family Bible; a small round table; a sweet little polished bookcase. The room might have had a certain elegance if it were not for the fact that my mother's older relatives had a habit of bequeathing their belongings, some to my grandmother, which all had to be accommodated. Consequently, during my childhood several more pieces of furniture were crammed into the room cheek by jowl with the other things and spoiled any impression of gracious living. Large ugly chests of drawers, pictures of unknown family members, sundry vases and knick-knacks, and worst of all, a collection of stuffed birds under glass domes. I hated seeing those birds, dead but artificially lifelike, with bright beady eyes, displayed for the interest of the curious. After a while they mysteriously disappeared; maybe our elders felt the same.

The parlour was not lived in on a daily basis or even entered much; a fire was lit on Sundays and we repaired there after Sunday dinner, to read and have our tea and spend a cosy evening, lit by an oil lamp, or later, by a hideous hissing Tilley lamp that gave out a bright white light that must have been better for our eyesight but very unflattering to the complexion.

Christmases were spent there too, and, of course, any time we expected visitors. It was a pleasant, spacious room and I wish we had spent more time there.

Back through the hall into the kitchen and through another of the five doors that would lead us to the stairs, bare wood with a bend in the middle. A small landing at the top with a linen cupboard, then a door to the left led to one bedroom and one to the right to the other two. The end bedroom to the right could be accessed only by walking through the middle one. This end room had a good-sized window in the gable end; the windows in the other two were at floor level under the eaves. The middle room was the largest, with plenty of room for two double beds, a wardrobe, washstand and various chests of drawers, with a shiny yellow linoleum patterned with rosebuds on the floor and sheepskin rugs beside the beds. I slept in this room for all of my childhood, sharing mostly with my aunt but sometimes a sibling. Our sleeping arrangements were somewhat haphazard, depending on who had recently died, been born, left home temporarily, or required special nursing. My grandmother occupied the end room until her death when I was eleven, my parents the room at the other end; Auntie sometimes left for a while to care for some relative in need, or a confinement or an illness. All the beds were high, metal-framed, double size, even the ones singly occupied, with a flock mattress topped by a feather bed, feather pillows, flannelette sheets, blankets and eiderdowns. Whatever the weather, we slept in warm cocoons.

Going down the stairs again, there was a window with a wide sill and a shelf opposite holding, among other things, the first aid cabinet, well out of the way of small fingers. As we turned the bend, the wall opposite held a huge map of the world with pictures of children of the nations all around the edges, entitled 'Heirs of the nations who will inherit the world of tomorrow'. I think this might have been published after World War 1, when there was a hopeful feeling of optimism throughout the world. This fascinated me, and I learned a lot of geography from loitering on the stairs and studying it.

One thing our house did not have was a bathroom, or even the luxury of hot water on tap. We washed in the back kitchen or from the jugs and basins on our washstands, and bathed in a galvanised tin tub in front of the kitchen fire, cosily screened by clothes horses warming our towels and pyjamas. Chamber pots under every bed provided for our night-time needs; by day we used the very rustic outhouse, shaded by a lilac tree, at the bottom of our garden. To reach it required trudging across the farmyard and down a narrow winding path fringed by shrubs and tall perennials. In the winter, when the dusty yard turned to mud, the trip required a coat, hat and Wellington boots, with a torch if darkness had fallen. It was a scary experience in the dark, with the shrubs casting dark shadows and brushing one with wet leaves if it was raining, bringing fears of lurking unknown things. Emerging from the outhouse, I would fix my eyes on the light in the kitchen window and run up the path to safety as fast as I could.

Our house was in many ways rustic, basic and even primitive, but we felt no sense of deprivation. Even when I gradually learned that other people had electric lighting, flushing indoor toilets, gleaming bathrooms and other mod cons, I wouldn't have changed places for anything. I was safe and secure and loved in our house. It was home.

CHAPTER FIVE

The Farm

Oh give me land, lots of land, under starry skies above, don't fence me in.

Cole Porter

I like space. I like vistas of fields and hills, mountains and woodland. I like dark skies with no artificial light, to be able to see the stars. I don't like looking out at walls and houses. I like fresh air and room to breathe it, trees with green leaves and waving branches, stillness and quiet.

We had all that in spades when I was a child. A hundred and eighteen acres of farmland, fields and woods, hedgerows and streams, and the freedom to go anywhere we liked as long as we remembered to close gates after us, and if we must climb them instead of going through, to do so at the hinge end. We had to respect livestock and not trample on growing crops

The farm for the most part was light-coloured medium loam, easy to work and dry, apart from a few boggy places. One wet field had been drained shortly after the war; there was another damp boggy place in the meadow below us, where rushes and globe flowers, wild orchids and blue scabious flourished, and curlews and peewits liked to nest. Like most in our area, my father kept a mixed farm, arable and pasture; sheep, cattle and crops of hay and corn. Unlike most, he was also something of a visionary and entrepreneur; he studied farming journals and sometimes broke away from the traditional breeds and methods. At one time he decided that a Border Leicester strain would be good to introduce to his flock of Cheviot ewes, creating Scottish Half-Breds, which produced a good crop of wool and were tough and hardy. So off he went to the sheep sales at Castle Douglas in the Scottish borders to purchase rams (or 'tups' as we knew them), large snooty-looking creatures with aristocratic Roman-nosed white faces.

Another time, he decided to introduce Galloway cattle into the area, a hardy Scottish beef breed, able to survive in the worst of winter conditions, excellent for beef and good for breeding. That time his search took him to Andover in Hampshire, where he was entertained by a prominent breeder who, I think, had a title, and where a butler waited upon them at dinner. In due course, a pedigree herd of black Galloways was installed, with long titles of their own in the pedigree herd book. There was a bull whose shortened name was Raven, who was of uncertain temper and could only be handled by my father. I am deeply ashamed to admit that more than once we exacerbated his bad temper by going into the feeding range next to Raven's stall and poking sticks at him through the partition to make him butt his head against the manger. Fortunately, the Galloway herd did not have horns; the cows were excellent and protective mothers and when they had calves, often fierce and unpredictable.

These new breeds, to my recollection, were not quite a failure and not quite a success. I don't think they caught on in the way my father had hoped and intended. As my brother remarked many years later, our dad and his ideas were somewhat ahead of his time.

Many years later, married to a farmer myself, a little town boy visitor to our all-arable farm looked round our empty yard in disappointment and exclaimed, 'I thought it was going to be a real farm!'

My childhood home was a real farm. As well as the cattle and sheep, we had a pig that grunted, ducks that quacked, hens that clucked, geese that hissed, not to mention the barking dog and meowing cats. We measured up to Old MacDonald's farm any day. All of these creatures passed through our farmyard every day about their own business. In consequence, there was a great deal of mud and muck, not that it bothered us children a jot. We were used to living our outdoor lives in wellies.

The farm buildings clustered around the house to the right and left – I'm so glad that whoever built the house left a view clear across the valley to those blue mountains towering like guardians along the opposite side. The house was built into a bank, so that the walls at the back were much lower, low enough for us to scramble on to the shingled roof of the back kitchen and dairy. To the right, opposite the back door, was a stone building with a loft above, and below, stables with hitching posts and stalls. I liked to hang upside down from the horizontal rail and fancy myself a trapeze artist. Our last carthorse, Captain, occupied this stable while he lived. Before him, when I was very small, had been Ruby, a very matronly brown horse on whose rolling back I used to ride in front of my father in my toddler days. There was another, livelier, friskier horse for a while; I think she was a lighter kind of breed or maybe a cross; in any case, she didn't work well between the shafts and wasn't there long. I used to love watching my father harnessing the horse for work, talking soothingly to it all the time, each piece in its turn. First the bit, the bridle with blinkers to keep sudden movements from startling the horse, the huge neck collar, the ridged wooden 'saddle', so different from a riding saddle, the girth, the hames, the breeching, the crupper. My father was good with horses and preferred them, I think, to machines. He was patient and kind with them, and they responded. I loved the smell of horse, the creak of leather, the brightness of the brasses, the jingle of harness. And later, an eager reader of pony books, I longed passionately for a pony of my own. I never got one; a pony was a luxury we simply could not afford, needing to be fed and not producing anything in return. At one time I began saving my sixpence a week pocket money (which dropped to threepence when times were hard) but gave up when I calculated that I would be in my forties before I had enough and by then, I thought, I'd be far too old to care. So I shed many tears and had to content myself with riding other people's ponies whenever I could. And later still, I sometimes rode Captain bareback, even occasionally coaxing him to a gallop, which got him into a lather and was frowned upon. One time I fell off and landed painfully on a pile of stones beside the road. I groomed and curry-combed the poor horse for hours, but he was sweet-natured and patient with me and put up with it all in good humour.

Next to the stable was a dim windowless building called the oil-house, full of big drums of engine oil, that held no interest for me at all. Neither did the loft space above, reached by outside stone steps, where poisonous substances were kept – sheep dip, strychnine and suchlike. Across the yard, skirting the garden wall, one came first to a couple of pigsties, one housing the current porker and one the home of the ducks. Next to them, with adjacent mixen (midden) came a row of cowsheds, or 'beast-houses' as they were sometimes called, with hay-lofts over and feeding ranges along the back of the stalls. Here the cows came in every day, to be milked and to suckle their calves, each going to her own stall and waiting to be secured with the metal chain ties. They munched on hay as the milking went on, while their calves bawled from an adjoining pen, impatient for their turn. At the very end was the bull pen with the granary over, also accessed by a flight of stone steps outside. Those steps could be slippery in wet or icy weather, I remember at least once slipping and tumbling down with my life flashing before my eyes.

At right angles to the cowshed, to the left of the house was another run of buildings housing young cattle, from there up steps to the 'engine-house' with the goose-shed nearby, and then to the big barn. Beyond that, up on the bank, was another lean-to shed which was the home of an ancient car, a Morris Oxford Bullnose, left behind by the Price family for some reason. Probably they just hadn't the room for it. All through my childhood the car never came out of the shed; it just stood there, brown and square and solid, gathering dust, providing perching places for hens and a play space for us children who liked to open the doors, get in and pretend-drive or honk the horn or play house on the leather seats. Today it would probably be worth a small fortune.

At the back of the barn was the rick-yard, with an open French barn for hay and straw, and below, down the slope behind the cowsheds, the orchard, a pleasant spot with old apple trees and a swing on a big branch. Around and beyond the buildings stretched the fields, large and small, reaching out in every direction. Some had to be accessed by crossing the public road, which we called going to the 'other side'. Most of them had names, some obvious or related to other farms or cottages in their vicinity. There were the Tynessa meadows, upper and lower, the field-above-the-house, the-field-below-the-house, Sunnybank, Wernypentre Field, Tall Trees, the Beech Field, the Hill (a flat field). But I never knew the origins of Lower Betyn and Upper Betyn.

It would be an exaggeration to say I knew every stick and stone of the place, but I had a pretty good knowledge of most of it; the individual trees and bushes, the thin places in the hedgerows (not many of those as my dad was an expert hedger), the banks where you'd find the first primroses and cowslips, the bushes that grew the juiciest blackberries, the trees that had good branches for climbing and building in. We had few constraints and lots of freedom. I don't think our parents were ever overly anxious about our whereabouts. They knew that our stomachs could be relied upon to tell us when it was time to head homeward.

CHAPTER SIX

The Food We Ate

Most of us have fond memories of food from our childhood.
Whether it was our mom's homemade lasagne or a memorable
chocolate birthday cake, food has a way of transporting us
back to the past.

Homaro Cantu

ationing was in full swing when I was born, and carried on when the war ended. Petrol had been the first commodity to be rationed early on, followed in January 1940 by rationing of bacon, butter and sugar. Soon meat, eggs, tea, jam, biscuits, breakfast cereals, cheese, lard, milk, canned and dried fruit, and soap had been added to the list. By August 1942 almost all foodstuffs were rationed, with the exception of vegetables and bread. Most fresh fruit was not rationed, but supplies were limited. Britishers were encouraged to cultivate their own plots for growing food, urged on by the popular slogan 'Dig for Victory'.

Rationing did not end with the ending of the war; in fact, some aspects became even stricter for some time and made the struggles of British housewives to feed their families even more difficult. Commodities were restored very gradually through the late forties and early fifties, but rationing was not officially ended until 1954. Britain was on its knees when the war ended; people had a tough time and often there was real hunger.

All of us had ration books, buff-coloured for an adult, green for a child under five. I believe there were also blue books for older children. It's the green ones I remember best. The Government strove to keep the children of Britain healthy by issuing free dietary supplements; concentrated orange juice and cod liver oil. Both came in flat-sided bottles about the same size. My mother from time to time added to these various other supplements; there was extract of malt in a big brown jar, toffee-flavoured and delicious. The orange juice was acceptable, the cod liver oil, administered on a teaspoon, not so much. It tasted horrible and smelt worse if you happened to dribble or spill some on your clothing.

Living on a farm meant that we were hugely advantaged as far as food was concerned. We were almost self-sufficient. Our cows provided milk, cream and butter. The pigs kept us supplied with pork, bacon and ham. There were hens and ducks who donated us their eggs and occasionally ended up in the pot themselves. We grew potatoes, swedes, turnips, beans, peas, cabbage, onions and salad greens and anything else that could be grown.

We had fruit trees, apples, plums, raspberries, strawberries, black and red currants; blackberries grew in the hedgerows and provided their free bounty for the picking. My mother bottled and preserved and pickled, and made jams and chutneys and marmalade. She made cakes, pies, puddings, tarts and most other things that could be home produced. Our grocery list was mostly bread (some of our neighbours made bread but, for some reason, our bread oven was never used), flour, sugar, dried fruit, candles, paraffin for heating, matches, coffee (mostly chicory-based coffee substitute), tea, cocoa, margarine, spices.

When goods began to trickle back into the shops, many children experienced new tastes for the first time. Many people remembered bananas as the first fruit to return, and I believe there was an official 'banana day' when each child in Britain received a banana. I don't remember my first banana, but I do remember the first processed jelly we'd ever seen. My mother had made it in a castle-shaped mould and brought it to the table on a plate in all its glory, green, wobbly and glistening. We were awestruck.

Breakfast cereals had less variety than they do nowadays. In our house it was mainly a choice of Weetabix or Shredded Wheat. We always had them with hot milk. Sometimes my mother made porridge, cooking it in a double saucepan to prevent sticking and burning; she'd put it on to cook and then have to leave it while she went out to do the milking. Boiled eggs were a favourite; I liked mine hard-boiled and still do. The adults sometimes had duck eggs, larger than hens' and pale green coloured. I tried them but didn't like the stronger taste.

Dinner was the main meal of the day and was eaten around 1pm. Bacon and ham were a staple in our diet, boiled, baked or fried. So was chicken, although if my mother had decided to get rid of an old hen who no longer laid, it often had to be boiled before it was roasted. Beef and mutton were less often consumed. My mother could make a great mutton stew with doughballs though, and her roast beef dinners were wonderful. Often vegetables were cooked in the same pot as ham or bacon, and sometimes even the pudding too, in a basin tied up in a pudding cloth. Rabbit played a big part in our wartime diets, as in the diets of many others. My mother would soak the skinned and gutted carcase, pink and shiny, overnight, and next day would stuff it with sage and onion to roast, or make a rabbit stew or a pie. The meat was there for the catching, highly nutritious and an important source of protein. Very tasty too. The only hazard was the odd piece of lead shot that was sometimes overlooked and came up on your plate or even in your mouth.

The vegetables we ate were picked from the garden on the same day, super fresh. Early summer was the best time for fresh veg, new potatoes, new peas, tender lettuce and radish and spring onions. Fish was a rarer alternative to meat, although sometimes we had fresh cod or haddock from the fishmonger in town.

And then there were the puddings. Apple tarts with cinnamon, rice pudding with sultanas, boiled puddings with Lyle's Golden Syrup cascading down their sides, roly-polies, pink blancmange, custard tart sprinkled with nutmeg, pancakes, stewed fruit. Stewed prunes seemed often on the menu, maybe for the good of our digestive systems. Custard with everything. Or in summer, strawberries with thick cream. How the farmers went back to work laden down with such solid fare beats me. But my dad, at least, never gained an ounce. Hard work soon burned off the calories.

By five o clock, having worked off their dinners, everyone was ready for tea. There'd be bread and butter, which we had to eat first before cake, jam, cheese, fruit cake, apple tart. On weekdays the cake was a plainish cut-and-come-again type, on Sundays we might have a fancier one with more fruit and cherries, or a Victoria sponge. Numerous cups of tea to wash it all down. In winter we had the pleasures of comfort foods. A pile of toast browned at the fire on a long toasting fork, buttered and stacked on a plate on the hob to keep warm, with the butter oozing down to a golden pool around the bottom slice. Crumpets sometimes. Welsh cakes, with plenty of currants, fried golden-brown on the griddle pan. And if there'd been a butter-making, we had fresh farm butter on crusty bread, or buttermilk cakes, beaten into a batter like pancakes and cooked in the big pan, spread with jam or syrup.

Supper was something of a moveable feast, and not optional. We didn't sit around the table all together as we did for dinner and tea. I think people ate if they were hungry, whatever was available, sitting round the fire. There were night-time beverages, Horlicks, cocoa or Ovaltine. As small children we sometimes had a bowl of bread broken up into hot milk, a comforting thing to go to bed on.

CHAPTER SEVEN

The Clothes We Wore

Sweater, n. garment worn by a child when its mother is feeling chilly.

Ambrose Bierce

My mother, in her heyday, so she gave me to understand, had been rather stylish and interested in fashion. The earliest pictures I have of her show a fair-haired child with large soulful eyes, in a dark dress and a starched and frilled white pinafore, with black stockings and buttoned boots. I also have a picture of her as a young woman in a loose, shapeless, flapper-style dress with a belt round the hips and shingled hair.

By the time the Great War of 1914-1918 ended, the world had changed rapidly; with the twenties and thirties came a revolution in women's clothing as in many other things. Gone were the long skirts and hampering layers of petticoats, the stays and corsets, the parasols and piled hair; in were the new women with short skirts, boyish figures, cropped hair and strappy shoes. My mother, as a modern young woman, was the proud possessor of a trendy blue three-piece beach set, consisting of a sun-top, shorts and a wraparound skirt. We have postcards sent from her to her family from seaside resorts as far apart as Aberystwyth and Dorchester and the North Yorkshire coast. I have a feeling she probably accompanied an aunt or some other relative on these holidays.

Following the advent of the War, clothing rationing began in June 1941, mainly to safeguard materials and concentrate on war production. Each type of clothing had a 'points' system depending on the amount of material and labour needed for its production. Eleven points were needed for a dress, two for a pair of stockings, eight for a man's shirt or pair of trousers. A set number of points were allocated to each person annually, and money as well as points needed to make purchases. Children's clothes had priority, and housewives were urged to 'Make Do and Mend', another encouraging slogan of the war years. Consequently, fashions in the war years had emphasis on using less material, and tended to be shorter and skimpier.

In my infant years, my mother's winter coat was a shortish, close-fitting garment of grey boucle material with a soft grey fur collar, which I think may have been rabbit fur. She always wore kid gloves; I believe there was a grey pair to match the coat. Later, when the war had ended and goods were no longer in such short supply, she splashed out on a new coat, this time fitted to the waist and flaring out into a longer wide skirt, the 'New Look'. This one was grey too, two tones in a soft herringbone weave. I thought she looked very smart in it. In summer my mother wore gauzy, flowered dresses for 'best', and for in between seasons, a suit (or costume) of navy blue or tweed. Her workaday wear was much more plebeian; an old jumper and skirt covered by a wrap-around pinafore, and often, over that, for dirty jobs like blackleading the grate or plucking and dressing poultry, a 'coarse apron' of Hessian sacking. When I was little, though, I remember her best in bib and brace dungarees, khaki land girl style, with a belt around the waist, for working with my dad on the farm. In later years, my mother adopted the polyester and Crimplene of the day, as did most women of her age, no doubt appreciating the easy-care qualities. She did have one elegant outfit that perfectly suited her, a fitted navy coat worn with a wide-brimmed navy hat. Hats were always worn during my childhood, though I can't remember much about them, except that hat pins were sometimes thrust through the hat and anchored to the hair on windy days.

My father liked to dress impressively too, and well-tailored clothes looked good on his 6'3" lean upright frame. For his wedding he had a three-piece suit of a smooth tweed, with a waistcoat and watch and chain. Both my parents rarely wore off-the-peg clothing; whenever they could afford it, they acquired tailored made-to-measure outfits, bringing home 'patterns' of fabric to discuss and pore over and look at in all kinds of lights. My father had a suit of lovat-green on one occasion; my mother's suits sometimes came with two skirts in different styles. Both liked subtle tweeds. These purchases were made to last and it was just as well; I don't think they could afford to splash out very often. My dad had a collection of hats in hatboxes; a bowler for occasions such as funerals, several trilbies and a straw boater for shade when the sun shone. I have the boater still, have tried wearing it myself and found it a very hard and uncomfortable piece of headgear. For work, my father invariably wore old collarless shirts and trousers under bib-and-brace overalls, his were a faded navy-blue, a flat cap, greasy with much wear, tattered jacket and Wellingtons. He had a big trench-coat type mackintosh for wet days.

Babies, boys and girls, wore long nightgowns made of a soft flannel, with maybe a matinee jacket over it. They had little wrap-around vests tied with ribbons, and terry nappies. I'm not sure when plastic pants came into use, but the early ones were rather horrid; after a few washes they became stiff and unpleasantly yellow-tinged. After a few months little girls went into short, smocked dresses and boys into rompers – virtually the same garment except that the boys' had elasticated legs and buttons to fasten underneath. Babies wore bonnets, bootees and various knitted garments. They were cocooned in shawls, hand-knitted or crocheted by doting grannies and aunties.

When I'd passed the toddler stage, I wore cotton dresses, sewed at home, and woollen cardigans, also hand-knitted by my mum and Auntie. Underwear consisted of interlock vests, with pants of the same for boys and navy blue knickers for girls, bloomer-style with elasticated legs and sometimes a little pocket for a handkerchief. I also had an undergarment called a liberty bodice, a garment designed, I believe, for ladies to be released from the bondage of the corset, which had dominated the world of the female undergarment for many decades. Small girls wore them too. It was a soft, shaped garment with fastenings up the front and sometimes attachments at the lower end for suspenders. I'm not sure whether it was intended to replace or in addition to a vest. Knowing my mother, who liked to keep us well-wrapped, it was the latter. It must have been a great relief for the formerly corseted ladies, some of whom had squeezed their waistlines into an 18" measurement. My mother wore a corset for all of her adult life until her death in 1985, though by then they were modified versions and more comfortable to wear. I wore a surgical corset for a short while after a back injury, and it was so excruciatingly un-comfortable that it almost made me forget the back pain. Maybe that was its purpose.

In winter I had pleated skirts, either on an attached cotton bodice or with shoulder straps that crossed at the back, and knitted jumpers. My brother wore grey flannel shorts with braces, and a jersey or a shirt with a sleeveless knitted pullover. Both of us had Clarks sturdy brown leather sandals with crepe soles and the familiar petal-shaped cut-out and T-straps for summer wear. In winter we were shod with sturdy boots and thick woollen socks that reached the knees and were secured in place with elastic garters. Little boys of toddler age wore long trousers; little girls had garments called legginettes, close filling jersey trousers that extended over the instep and had elastic stirrup straps underneath to keep them in place. Once past the toddler age, girls no longer wore trousers and boys had knee-length shorts until about fourteen or so when they went into 'longs'. Consequently, although we were always cocooned in winter in woollen coats, hats, scarves, gloves and boots, our knees were always bare to the elements, even in the most bitter weather. Hardly any wonder that they were often red, sore and chapped, and whatever the season, were always decorated with scabs, scrapes and bruises from falls and bumps. We also often had a sore red circle round our legs where the wellies rubbed and chafed.

When we somehow gained the knowledge that in America the children, boys and girls, wore blue jeans, I longed for them with a passion. I begged and pleaded with my poor mother, who had no idea where such items could be obtained until in desperation she ran me up a pair of khaki drill trousers with elastic round the waist. They were somewhat shapeless and far from the pictures of jeans I'd seen, but they were trousers and for the moment they sufficed.

For school I had the pleated pinafore-style garment known as a gym slip, held in by a girdle at the waist. I also had a school mac, brown gaberdine, that seemed to last year after year – it had a checked lining to the hood but the name Burberry meant nothing to me. Our winter coats were tweedy wool mixtures, belted for the boys, rather daintier and more fitted for girls. I also had a 'best' winter dress made to measure from some fine wool cloth my mum had been hoarding for years. It was soft and warm, the style was pretty, with a fitted top, belt at the waist and a pleated skirt, but I disliked it because of the colour, a particularly bright, lurid shade of magenta. I'm sure it did nothing for my pale complexion, but the colour was incidental; good material was good material and we must make the best use of it.

CHAPTER EIGHT

School

Instruction does much, but encouragement everything.

J.W. Goethe

I started school later than most, at six years and nine months to be precise. The village school in Clyro was two and a half miles away, we had no car at that time and there was no school transport. It would mean a round trip of five miles, the return journey uphill all the way, a long walk for little legs. Many farm children did walk long distances to school; my mother, however, decided that hers would not. With other parents, she and my father applied for transport and eventually got it. My brother was just five, school-starting age. I had already learned to read and write, with the help of the adults in the house, so would not be at a disadvantage.

We were told one Saturday morning in October, the news probably having been delivered by Mr Evans the postman, that a school car would stop at our road gate and transport us to school on Monday morning. Our response was to sit down side by side on the sofa and howl in unison. I was heartbroken. I did not want to go to school or see the need. My little world seemed to have come to an end, its foundations shattered. I didn't want to go.

Monday morning duly arrived and to school we went, piling into Bill Powell's Austin taxi. My mother came with us that first morning, ever protective. It must have been a pleasant autumn day, because I wore a blue cotton dress patterned with white flowers and a pale yellow cardigan, both made by my mother, my hair plaited tightly in pigtails and fastened with ribbons. I remember my brother's sad, worried little face. There were others in the car, children of neighbouring farmers; I was far too shy to speak to them or even look at their faces. No other parents. All the children were rather solemn at this momentous experience. My mother went into school surrounded by half a dozen children. I have no memory of what happened that first morning. My mother must have stayed to get us all registered, because she later told us that one little girl was so overcome, she could only speak in a whisper. She was asked her father's full name and whispered, 'Mr Prosser.' The headmaster, wanting his Christian name, asked, 'Well, what does your mother call him?' The whisper came again, 'Mr Prosser.'

We must have settled well because we went willingly to school from then on, transported thence by Mr Powell. He was a faithful, fatherly figure although he had no wife or child of his own, and took the greatest care of us all. I believe he could be a bit grumpy if adults kept him waiting, but he was always kind to us children. His greeting to us in the morning never varied, it was always a cheerful 'Morning, Eleanor and Ron!' In the afternoons he dropped us off with the familiar refrain of 'So long, Eleanor and Ron!' On the occasions we were late, he would wait patiently at the gate for us to come. Those latenesses were a source of real embarrassment to me; coming across the field and seeing the car waiting, we would break into a run, with several interested faces peering at us from the car windows and my face scarlet with mortification. Mr Powell never reproached us. A former fellow traveller recently told me that once, with snow thick on the ground, Mr Powell had carried her to the car. The journey itself was pleasantly relaxing and leisurely; we stopped at the appointed places to pick up others and noted anything of interest along the way. There was no bypass then, so our route meandered through the village and almost every day we encountered the herd of milking cows being driven out to pasture from Ashbrook Farm, which stood where Clyro Garage stands now, causing a welcome few minutes' delay while they passed. On the way home, the same thing invariably happened in reverse, as they were brought back for the evening milking.

I started off with my brother in the Infants Class, taught by Miss Ethel Anthony, a well-corseted, well-dressed single lady from the village. I thought her very old, but she was probably somewhere in her forties then. Miss Anthony kept strict order and had a stern demeanour, but we instinctively knew that she had a kind heart. She also had a good sense of humour that showed itself from time to time. Miss Anthony was part of the Anthony clan, a large family that occupied several homes in a terrace in the village. Her brother Bill was a carpenter; he and his wife had a large family of nine red-headed children, all of whom passed through the school in their turn. A popular good-looking family, some of them and their descendants remain in the village today.

I didn't stay long in Miss Anthony's class but in a short time was promoted to the Top Class, where I remained for the rest of my time in primary school. There were just the two classes then; later a third classroom was installed between the others, appropriately named the Middle Class.

The Top Class was a large room, heated in winter by a stove that burned coke. I'd never heard of coke before; coal I knew, and I decided that coke must be a posher name for coal. I tried to instruct my parents in the correct pronunciation; I'm sure they put me straight on that. We sat at wooden desks with attached seats, in blocks of two. The desks had lift-up lids for our books, an indented groove in the lid for pencils and pens, and a sunken built-in inkwell. We wrote mostly in pencil, I think; the steel pens were unreliable things, having to be constantly dipped in ink and likely to leave many blots and smudges, the nibs troublesome and given to the two points crossing if one bore down too hard. The desk lids bore signs of use and abuse with ink-stains, initials, dents and even attempts at illicit carvings of names.

The headmaster taught the Top Class, Mr Bennet, a tall, thin, rather stooped man with spectacles, who wore a black beret, Breton-style. I have only vague memories of him. I have a feeling he was rather vague and absent-minded himself, on the verge of retirement. He taught us reading and sums, anything else escapes me, though the vicar, the Rev. Lloyd, came in some mornings a week for Scripture lessons. We had prayers every morning with the whole school, little ones in front. I remember turning my head to look in awe at the big girls in the back row, Joan Harley, Monica Gell, Bessie and Margaret Thomas – big strapping girls of ten and eleven, towering over us little ones.

A breath of fresh air seemed to sweep into the school when Mr Bennet retired and we got a new headmaster, a much younger man, Mr Evans. Mr Evans was from Newport and had a wife and a daughter a little older than me. His younger daughter was born a few years later, a little before the birth of our younger brother Tim. Mr Evans and his family lived in the school house next door to the school. He introduced new ideas and innovations to the school and it became much more lively and interesting. He set up a percussion band, furnishing us with a variety of triangles, castanets, cymbals, tambourines and drums, the sound of which I'm sure must have been horribly discordant and raucous most of the time but which we enjoyed enormously. We listened to radio programmes for schools. I remember the music ones best; *Singing Together* on a Monday,

Rhythm and Melody on a Thursday. We learned a great many folk songs from all over the world and I could sing them all now; *Camptown Races, There's a Hole in My Bucket, Sourwood Mountain, In Poland Stands an Inn, John Peel, Old Farmer Bunn* – there were many, many more. We listened to a radio production of *Peter and the Wolf* and performed our own version, matching our percussion instruments to the characters. We went on nature walks in all weathers, splashing through the puddles on wet days, collecting specimens for future study. We had the sticky buds of horse chestnuts bursting into leaf on our classroom windowsill, along with frogspawn in glass containers where we could watch it morphing into wiggly tadpoles and then little frogs. We grew mustard and cress from seeds on damp blotting paper. We had a grounding in science. Mr Evans kept a tube of mercury in his desk, and from time to time, he would tip it out and let us watch the way it rolled apart and then together, fluid but not really a liquid. We were allowed to prod and manipulate it to make it move, and I have a feeling we did it with our bare fingers! I could be wrong there, but if not, I hope we washed our hands afterwards. We had our daily quota of milk at break time, in little bottles containing one third of a pint, with a straw to drink it and much slurping when we got to the bottom of the bottle. At dinner time we left the school yard and walked in a crocodile towards the village to the Church Hall, called then the Assembly Rooms, and had our cooked lunch. One child was designated dinner monitor of the day, and sallied forth during the morning to tell the cooks how many dinners would be required that day. Depending on how keen you were on lessons, you hurried back along the pavement or took your time.

Mr Evans made lessons interesting. He subscribed to an educational magazine and would sometimes bring a copy into class and read us a story from it. The look of the shiny paper, the black print, the crackle as he turned back the page, gave me a strange feeling I've never forgotten – hard to explain, a mixture of anticipation, excitement and wonder that almost gave me shivers down my spine. That magazine held a kind of promise to me every time.

The school stood at the fork in the village where two roads diverged, one going to Hay-on-Wye, the other to Llowes and Glasbury. It was (and still is, though no longer a school) a long, one-storey building with two porched entrances, one for the boys and one for the girls, where we lined up in our appropriate queues when it was time to enter. At each side was a well-worn path round to 'the back' where stood a row of small toilets, one row for boys and one for girls, and woe betide any hapless infant who accidentally visited the wrong one! In the porches we divested ourselves of coats, hats, scarves and wellies, if we'd brought indoor footwear with us. Many did not and wore their wellies all day. The playground was hard-surfaced, surrounded by metal railings with a small gate at one end for pedestrians and, I think, a bigger gate at the other side for vehicle access if needed. I had an unfortunate encounter with those railings one day, when a group of us girls were playing some silly game which involved linking arms, closing our eyes and swooping blindly and aimlessly in all directions. My swooping led my face into close contact with the rails, and I damaged two front teeth. I was escorted to Mr Evans, where I tearfully told him that they were my 'new teeth'. He was sympathetic, but there wasn't a lot he could do. I imagine there were fairly frequent accidents in that playground; falls and contact with the hard surface would have resulted in cuts, bruises, scrapes, grazes and plenty of tears. Nobody ever got sent home in such circumstances; they were patched up and comforted and got on with the day.

I made friends at school. With my crippling childhood shyness, I would never make a leader, but I was often the best friend and sidekick of a leader. Through most of my days in Clyro Primary it was Sandra, an only child, pretty, confident, bright and possessing a kind of sophistication that most of us farm girls lacked. I was also friendly with Amy Evans, the head's daughter. On one occasion the school was visited by an inspector, always an ordeal for everyone and looked forward to with dread. We were cautioned to be on our very best behaviour. Amy and I were sharing a desk, and the inspector asked one of us to stand up and recite something or other. Alas, we could not, or could not do so separately; in an idle moment while waiting to be inspected, we had whiled away the time by plaiting our long hair together.

Sandra and Amy both had strong personalities, which sometimes clashed and occasionally resulted in full-blown hair-pulling, scratching, screeching fights. I remember one such taking place on the steps of the girls' porch, and although not directly involved in the fight, we by-standers were hauled in front of the head as well as the culprits. I aligned myself strongly with Sandra, feeling that Mr Evans would surely be on the side of his daughter. Mr Evans must have read my mind, because he repeated to me word for word what I was thinking, gave me a good telling off and reduced me to tears. It must have been upsetting for him too, but it didn't stop it happening again.

We played skipping games, chanting games, hopscotch, games we made up ourselves, altering the rules as we went along to suit ourselves. Across the road was a line of tall trees where rooks nested, and the cawing of the rooks made a background to the noise and chatter of the playground. School was a happy place.

CHAPTER NINE

Church

The chapel of the Holy Trinity lies remote amongst its fields. The simple, single-cell building was rebuilt in 1878, but the fine medieval roof was reclaimed, together with part of a screen, and a font brought from Clyro.

from CPAT Radnorshire Churches Survey Project

*M*y family were Anglican – that is, my mother's side were faithful churchgoers, my father's not so much, although they would have categorised themselves as Church of England too. My mother and aunt went regularly to church and were faithful supporters of the Mother's Union and Women's Institute respectively. My grandmother, though in later years unable to attend church, observed the Sabbath by sitting by the parlour fire and reading the *Prayer Book* and her weekly copy of the *Christian Herald*. My father's church attendance was more sporadic; he may have gone to an Easter or Christmas service, but his main churchgoing, along with all the other farmers in the district, happened at Harvest Thanksgiving. On these occasions, the farming men never sat with their families, but clumped together in the back seats, a couple of rows of men freshly shaved and in their best suits and polished boots. I was proud that my father was the tallest man there and that he had the best (in my opinion) singing voice. He had a wonderful voice, deep and mellow, and he always took the bass part. I could easily pick out his voice as we sang the old familiar harvest hymns: *Come, Ye Thankful People, Come; O Lord of Earth and Sky and Sea;* and, in particular…

> *We plough the fields and scatter the good seed on the land*
> *But it is fed and watered by God's Almighty hand*
> *He sends the snow in winter, the warmth to swell the grain*
> *The breezes and the sunshine, and soft refreshing rain.*

All good gifts around us, are sent from Heav'n above
Then thank the Lord, oh thank the Lord, for a-a-all his love.

...which the men sang with all their hearts and souls, sending shivers up and down my spine.

Our church was rather unique and special, known as Bettws Chapel but actually the Anglican sister church to St Mary's in Clyro. Set down in an isolated spot in the middle of a field with no road access, it looked over the vistas of the Wye Valley. A simple, one-room structure with a curtained-off vestry at the back, it had been completely rebuilt in 1878 but retained the design and some of the original medieval materials. There was a bell turret at one end, lancet windows, whitewashed walls and rush-seated chairs. Services were fortnightly at 3pm and the church was well over a mile away from where we lived. Getting there was quite an adventure in itself as we travelled on foot and were not usually deterred by the weather, summer or winter. The diarist Francis Kilvert ministered there during his curacy at Clyro in the nineteenth century, and had even further to come, three miles from Clyro and uphill all the way. Weather did not deter him either. He writes on February 13th, 1870:

> *The weather fearful, violent deadly East wind and the hardest frost we have had yet. Went to Bettws in the afternoon, wrapped in two waistcoats, two coats, a muffler and a mackintosh and was not at all too warm. Heard the chapel bell pealing strongly for the second time since I have been here, and when I got to the chapel my beard, moustache and whiskers were so stiff with ice that I could hardly open my mouth, and my beard was frozen to my mackintosh.*

On January 1st, 1872, he writes:

> *Went to Bettws, the chapel bell tolled out sharp and sudden through the white mist ... the hedges were hoary with rime and frost, and the trees were hailing large pieces of ice down into the road. Few people in chapel...*

There were often few in our day too; going to a service at Bettws in the winter was not for the faint-hearted. We would eat our Sunday dinner, get dressed in our best, and set out on the long walk. The route began by leaving our back door and, instead of going ahead to the road gate as usual, taking a sharp turn to the right and skirting the hedge along the field above the house until we came to a stile leading into the 'Roughs'. The Roughs was not then part of our farm, but it was an acknowledged path to our destination. We loved the Roughs, a big rambling uncultivated area dotted with gorse and bramble bushes and hawthorns, and often sneaked there to play and explore and build dens in the tangled bushes.

In one corner stood the ruins of Whitehall, which had once been a substantial farmhouse with a wide grassy lawn. In its heyday, it had been a popular gathering place for social events. Kilvert writes on 3rd May 1870:

> *Poor Whitehall, sad, silent and lonely ... its cold chimney still ivy-clustered. I walked round and looked in at the broken, unframed windows and pushed open a door – which swung slowly and wearily together again. Here were held the Quarterly Dances. What fun! What merry-makings, the young people coming in couples and parties to dance in the long room. What laughing, flirting, joking and kissing behind the door or in the dark garden among the young folks, while the elders sat around the room with pipes and mugs of beer or cider from the 'Black Ox' of Coldbrook hard by. Now how all is changed, song and dance still, mirth fled away.*

Whitehall was already falling into disrepair in Kilvert's day; by our time, all that remained were roofless stone walls, some towering high with stones balancing precariously at the topmost point. More stones probably crashed down whenever there were high winds. We loved it, and liked to poke about the rooms and outbuildings to see what we could find. An old wagon stood in an outhouse, and in February the hedgerows around the lawn and gardens would be bordered by a nodding sea of beautiful white snowdrops. Just past Whitehall ran a green overgrown lane, the Coldbrook of Kilvert's day, part of the old drover's road and site of the Black Ox inn. We crossed the lane and climbed another stile into another field belonging to Penrheol a little further along, where an unofficial footpath ran through. Past a line of hawthorns, which in springtime would be frothy with sweet-smelling creamy Mayblossom, down a grassy hill to a hollow with a stream (I think there were stepping stones), up the other side and through a gate in the hedge that took us out onto a hard road. We turned right to head to church. At that point we were sometimes joined by Mrs Price, Pant-y-cae, who lived just across the lane. Occasionally she had her daughter Eileen with her. Eileen worked 'off' somewhere, was only home sometimes and seemed the height of fashion; she wore suits with tiny nipped-in waists, smart little hats, and shoes with heels and peep-toes, highly unsuitable for trudging muddy country roads, but to my child's eyes the height of elegance. The grown-ups exchanged news and gossip as we went on our way, joined at Penrheol by Mrs Greenway, a small, pale, quiet little lady, and at Llwyn Gwilliam turn by Mrs Layton and all or some of her four pretty daughters. From there we made our way in a body round the corner, through the gate on the right, down a track and finally through another gate on the left leading to the church. There was no road or pathway leading to the church – once a fortnight was not sufficient to make a track – and we walked though grass long or short, depending on the time of year and whether anyone had been mowing. It was often muddy too. If we had dallied too long on the way, the sound of the bell would hurry us up, and if it stopped ringing before we got there, we knew we were late.

Wellies, umbrellas and sometimes mackintoshes were shed in the porch but it was prudent to retain as much warm clothing as we could, the heating being from an oil stove and not always adequate. Inside, there'd be a sense of calm, our voices hushed. Mrs Watkins, Crossfoot would be playing the organ, a somewhat wheezy and antiquated instrument which she tackled bravely fortnight after fortnight. There might only be a handful of us, but no matter; where two or three are gathered together, the Lord is in their midst, and the vicar would always conduct a full service of Evening Worship from the Prayer Book for whoever came. The vicar at that time was the Rev. Lloyd, a gentle silver-haired saint who chanted the offices and responses and seemed kindly but slightly vague. He retired during my childhood and was replaced by the Rev. Lewis, a younger, larger and much more robust person with a good, loud speaking and singing voice; just as well, as we needed all the help we could get in that department. During the war years, we ended every service by singing *Eternal Father, Strong to Save*, remembering our army, our Air Force, and 'those in peril on the sea'. Later my mother told me that when we got to the lines, 'and bid'st the mighty ocean deep its own appointed limits keep,' my brother would substitute the word 'limpets'. Well, he might have been not much more than a toddler, but he knew that limpets were something to do with the sea, so it made perfect sense to him. I pondered the words of the Prayer Book as they were repeated, noting that a large part of it referred to the fact that Jesus died for the sins of the world, and puzzled over them – because already I knew that there were plenty of bad things, which must mean it hadn't worked very well. It wasn't until my teenage years that I came to understand that sin is a personal thing and must be dealt with in a personal way, each individual needing to accept forgiveness for him- or herself. But I am grateful for the familiar words of the Scriptures and the hymns; they may not have meant much at the time but came to mean a great deal later.

The collection bag would come round, carried by a volunteer from among us, and I would put in my penny. I thought a penny was what everyone put in and was rather impressed to discover that most of the grown-ups actually put in florins or half-crowns! The benediction would be given and we'd leave church, talking in a rather more subdued way than before, and make our way home, people dropping off as we came to their gates or lanes or yards. Mrs Watkins always had a lift to and from church with the vicar, but the rest of us meandered homeward to change from our best clothes and have Sunday tea, which was always fancier than the everyday one.

Sometimes visitors came on Sunday afternoons – usually relatives, aunts, uncles and cousins – and then tea would be even more special, with the best bone china, almost transparent white with a gold rim and delicate pattern of pink trailing roses and green leaves. My dad sometimes remarked that tea tasted better when drunk from bone china. Visitors meant best behaviour; respect for our elders, good manners and politeness were important to our mother and drummed into us from our infant years.

CHAPTER TEN

In Sickness and in Health

My own prescription for health is less paperwork and more
running barefoot through the grass.

Leslie Grimutter

My mother maintained that for the first two or three years of our lives, my brother and I were the pictures of health, robust, rosy-cheeked and sturdy. Whooping-cough in our toddler years put a stop to that.

Whooping-cough was a dangerous and debilitating illness in those days, before a vaccine had been found to prevent it or lessen its effects, with a pitiless wracking cough that gave the sufferer no rest and could take months to get rid of. My brother was particularly badly affected. I remember nothing of the illness, but my mother would relate how it had been.

'Many's the time,' she would declare with a touch of drama, 'that he would cough and cough and cough and then flop down on the bed all white and still, and we would think he had gone.'

They watched by our bedsides day and night for a long time, and we survived, but as changed infants. We emerged pale, thin and frail shadows of our former selves, and from then on were considered somewhat delicate. 'You were never the same again!' my mother would tell us tragically.

Whether to do with the whooping-cough or not, early in childhood I began to feel a strange tight sensation in my chest, almost a heavy lump, that made me feel I couldn't get my breath. It would persist for a few days or a week or so and then go away again. Various doctors were consulted, including a Dr Crawford, who I think perhaps was a school doctor, who came to our home at intervals to examine me. He at first suspected a type of asthma; I was, he said, a typical asthmatic child, nervous, sensitive and highly-strung; which diagnosis was accurate, but he was still at a loss because I did not have the typical wheezy breathing and cough of asthma sufferers. I had the symptoms on and off for several years before they finally stopped. We never knew the cause. It's been my opinion since that it was some kind of nervous reaction, or even an allergy. I have theories about the feather beds we slept on. I also had quite a bad attack of croup one time, and can remember the panic, the struggling for breath and the strange ringing cough. While my mother scurried around boiling kettles for inhaling steam, my father sat on the bed and held me, trying to reassure me. 'It's all right, darling. You'll be all right. Don't be frightened, darling. It will be better soon.' He never called me darling as a rule. I thought I must be dying, but felt strangely reassured.

Dr Crawford was a kindly, bespectacled man; he would peer down my throat and make me say, 'Aaaaarh!' or tap my chest and listen with his stethoscope while I repeated, 'Ninety-nine!' At one time he pondered the merits of sending me to an open-air school, but sensibly concluded that we had as much or more open-air living at home and told my mother to let us play outside as much as possible, barefoot if we liked. I'm not sure of the wisdom of that last instruction as regards a farmyard, but I'm so glad he didn't send me away. I would have been devastated.

Apparently, I also became fussy and finicky about the food I ate. When we started school, I did not like the school dinners, so my mother made an arrangement whereby I was served Oxo and bread instead. One of the school cooks, Mrs Webb, took a poor view of this fussiness and would thump the food down in front of me with a comment of 'There you are, Miss Finicky!' or something similar. She was smugly pleased when this arrangement came to an end. My mother, having decided I should eat school dinners like everyone else, visited the school again and Mrs Webb told me triumphantly, 'Your mother says you're to have school dinners again, so there.'

We had the usual childhood illnesses – chicken pox, mumps, coughs and colds. My parents were advised that our health would greatly benefit if our tonsils came out; it was a fashionable practice at that time to remove tonsils and often adenoids as well, healthy or not. So out ours had to come. News of the impending surgery was greeted with tears, pleadings and protests; which our elders tried to alleviate with promises of the jelly and ice-cream we would get afterwards, and a new book each! I remember the rubber mask over my face and waking to find myself in a ward full of children. To my dismay, my brother was in a bed at the very far end of the ward. After a day or two we were moved next to each other; the first thing we did was swap our new books, having read our own from cover to cover. We had our jelly and ice cream and we read our books. We were due to go home a few days later, but on that morning, I developed a mild fever and had to be kept in. I was desolate. That afternoon, I was visited by Aunt Rose Bracher, a cousin of my father's, a large imposing lady who lived in Hereford and was manageress of the fur department at Greenlands, the city's most exclusive store. She found me, a pathetic, sobbing, damp little heap huddled in the bed, and felt deeply sorry for me. Maybe it was that visit that nudged her into leaving us children a considerable amount (in those days) of money in her will, which came as a complete surprise seven or eight years later. That windfall was enough to furnish and carpet my house when I married and set up my own home. I was discharged next day and returned home to my feather bed and chicken soup and all the comforts of convalescence. Unfortunately, we picked up measles in the hospital and were quite poorly for some time, off school for the best part of half a term, if I remember rightly.

Illness could be quite enjoyable if it wasn't too painful or uncomfortable. A bad cold meant being tucked up in a cosy bed, with a hot water bottle if needed, and a good supply of books or comics. Big muslin squares, left from our baby days, were soft and comforting to runny sore noses, and we had hot drinks made from blackcurrant jam and honey in hot water. Camphorated oil rubbed on the chest gave off a pleasant medicinal smell and eased blocked tubes. We got special delicacies like jelly and home-made soup that would easily slip down a sore throat. We could ask for whatever food we fancied. If the weather was chilly, a little oil-stove would be lit in the bedroom, to 'take the chill off' as my mother would say. It was a tall, tubular white enamelled one with a fancy cut-out pattern in the top that gave out minimal heat but cast a pretty reflective pattern on the ceiling when it was dark and, along with the soft popping sound it made, was wonderfully comforting.

As well as the government-issued cod liver oil and orange juice, my mother was constantly on the lookout for other dietary supplements to 'build us up'. We loved the sticky, toffee-flavoured malt extract and ate it by the tablespoonful, but other substances were not as pleasant. There was Milk of Magnesia, a thick, white chalky mixture administered to help digestive problems; if that didn't work and constipation set in, there was always the dreaded Syrup of Figs. There was Vaseline to combat dryness and soreness. We had Owbridges Lung Tonic and Vicks vapour rub, Zubes lozenges to suck for a sore throat. These came in a round tin box with a horse on the lid and I think must have originated in America; their popular advertising slogan read something like, 'A little hoarse – go suck a Zube!' There was Friar's Balsam, which involved a towel over the head while inhaling hot steamy water to help clear blocked tubes. My mother was not averse either to using old-fashioned remedies; a sock (which had to have been worn by the patient that day) safety-pinned around the neck overnight to cure a sore throat, or goose grease applied both externally and internally. Cloves were good for toothache. Swellings or cuts that had become infected were sometimes treated with bread poultices to 'draw out' the poison. A lot of our cuts and scrapes did get infected, possibly due to close contact with a farmyard. There were no tetanus immunisations in those day; I'm surprised farm children managed to escape it. We had the vaccinations of the time; diphtheria and smallpox and that was about it.

The school doctor visited at intervals, examining every child in the school, stripped down to their underwear. In between, the nurse visited, to examine our hair for traces of nits. I had very long thick hair, but apparently no nit ever found a home in it. Maybe the classroom was too chilly for them to survive. Not so in later years, when my mother was told my younger brother had picked up an infestation. So ashamed was she that she travelled to another town on purpose to buy the prescribed potion in a place where no-one would know her.

The event of the school dentist was one that reduced us all to fear and trembling for days before it happened. Lurid tales flew about; he was reckoned to be a butcher as well as a dentist, which we half-believed and which struck terror into our hearts. The advent of anaesthetics instead of the dreaded 'needle' brought a wave of relief. With 'gas', you just went to sleep and when you woke it was all over. Tooth extractions seemed to be quite common; having a tooth out was preferable to having one filled, with all the drilling that caused excruciating pain if it touched a nerve.

In fact, I remember very little about the school dentist. What I do remember vividly is going to a dentist in Brecon, along with a whole lot of other children and their mothers, some of whom I recognised and some I didn't. We all sat in the waiting-room, silent and apprehensive, waiting our turn to be called in. All might have been well if one little girl, pushed to the limit of her self-control, suddenly lost it and burst into loud tears and wailing. The effects of the meltdown were immediate. In an instant, the whole waiting room was transformed into a tearful mass of sobbing, shrieking, wailing children, clinging to their mothers and pleading to be taken home. I do not know whether or not order was restored or whether we saw the dentist that day. Poor man, he must have had his work cut out. Thank goodness dentists are trained in methods of managing child patients these days.

We had our share of accidents, bumps and bruises, though I'm surprised there were never any broken bones, given our penchant for tree-climbing, scaling walls, climbing on roofs and occasionally flinging ourselves from upstairs windows in the house or buildings. I once fell off the back of a horse and landed painfully on one of the piles of stones that stood at intervals along our farm track, waiting for such time as they could be used for the construction of a hard road. No serious injury ensued, and I think I got back on the horse. When I was two, I'm told, I fell in the garden on to a piece of sharp slate that had been placed vertically to make an edging for a flower bed. I cut my left knee very badly; I don't know whether it was stitched or had any medical treatment, but I've had a small white mark there all my life. Another time, I was playing on the hearthrug, my mother, carrying a bowl of water from the boiler, tripped, and I was showered with near-boiling water over my back and shoulders. I was badly scalded, though I don't remember that either, but my mother was always filled with remorse when she talked about the incident.

All of us suffered from chilblains in the winter; no wonder, when we toasted our cold feet on the fender as near as we could get to the fire. We accepted them; they itched and burned but were part of the winter. We were never required, thank goodness, to try the remedy of threshing them with holly, which we were told was a recommended treatment. I also had warts on my hands and knees at one time: again, probably they were picked up from farm animals. Various remedies were tried, but they disappeared by themselves after a while and never returned.

Seeing our own GP was a nerve-wracking business too, unlike the school doctor, when everyone was in the same boat. You only went to the doctor if something was really wrong and all else had failed. And if he had to be called out, it was serious and might be a matter of life and death. My brother was really poorly with the measles and had a high fever. The doctor was called and I sobbed and cried, thinking he was going to die. My mother's way of managing fevers would be considered ill-advised today; her instinct was to keep the patient warm, so the feverish one would be smothered in extra quilts and blankets. If anyone had suggested then that a febrile child should be stripped, sponged with tepid water and cooled with a fan, she would have thrown up her hands in horror.

But we survived and we grew and thrived, and eventually left our childhood ailments behind.

CHAPTER ELEVEN

Communication

In an age like ours, which is not given to letter-writing, we
forget what an important part it used to play in people's lives.

Anatole Broyard

We didn't have a telephone. The nearest was half a mile away when I was small, a lone red kiosk standing at a crossroads. A tattered and well-thumbed directory sat on the shelf. You put in your coins, dialled and waited for the operator's voice, asking for the number you required. It was quite nerve-wracking, listening to the ring tone and wondering if the person would answer, and planning what you would say if they did. And wondering if the coinage clutched in your hand would be enough to continue the call when the pips warned that you had run out of time. My mother got quite stressed when she had to make a phone call; consequently, calls were only made in fairly dire circumstances.

Later, when the phone was installed at home, it started off as a party line and you sometimes heard snatches of other people's conversations when you picked up, or, maybe more worrying, you'd have the suspicion that someone else was listening in to yours.

Our main line of communication was the postal service, and the postman himself. Our postman was Mr Evans, moustached, bespectacled and getting on in years, or so it seemed to us. Mr Evans came, rain or shine, on his ancient but reliable bicycle with his bulging post-bag, on wet days wearing a voluminous waterproof cape over all. He lived at Paradise Cottage in the village, and not only delivered mail but also relayed verbally any message that needed to be sent to and from other places along his route. He never seemed in any great hurry and could be relied upon to know the latest bits of news and gossip.

We looked forward with great anticipation to the postman's visits, which usually happened about lunchtime or even later in the afternoon. Not only would there be the usual boring brown envelopes with typewritten address, indicating a bill or some business correspondence, but there might be a white envelope with the address handwritten, which was a real letter. Our relatives wrote quite regularly to one another, exchanging news, sharing family events – births, deaths, marriages – making arrangements to meet in town on Thursday, arranging visits. We had catalogues through the post, farming stuff, seed catalogues, and clothing and household items, notably J.D. Williams. My mother kept all the old clothing catalogues in a pile at one end on the mantelpiece, they were known as the 'fashion books', and I considered it a great treat to be allowed to get them down and leaf through them. When the Christmas season came around again, the gift catalogue was heralded with delight and seized upon; we were allowed to choose, within reason, our main present. Not that our choice was unlimited. For a few years I longed for a mechanical ride-on horse called a Mobo Bronco; if I couldn't have a real pony this seemed to be the next best thing. But it was far too expensive and out of our reach.

For years Ron and I received and pored over a joke and novelty catalogue called *Ellisdons*, and every year sent in an order, along with the necessary postal order, for such ridiculous and pointless things as whoopee cushions, itching powder, buttonholes that squirted water into your face, soap that made your face black when you washed with it, and a wonderful gadget called the SeeBackrosCope, which enabled you to see behind you when you peered into it. I did not like the shape of my nose, and once acquired from *Ellisdons* a contraption of stiff board and string to tie in place over that feature, which was supposed to alter its shape. The trouble was I could only wear it in absolute secrecy because I knew the teasing I'd get, so maybe that's why it didn't work.

We wrote letters from an early age. 'Thank you' letters after Christmas and birthdays were mandatory, and we also wrote to our Granny Francis and sundry other relatives at other times of the year. My parents both communicated with their families by letter, both of them writing in the beautiful copperplate style they'd been taught at school. If they were apart for any reason, which didn't happen very often, they wrote letters to each other. During wartime and rationing, paper was in short supply, so every scrap of space must be used up, lines close together and often continuing around the margins. In my parents' younger days, black-edged stationery was still used if there had been a death in the family. Postcards were eagerly perused, especially from holiday destinations, although the messages were usually brief; there was a theory that the postal people read all the postcards.

Mr Evans also delivered other things, parcels of all shapes and sizes, always thrilling but often disappointing as they were most likely to contain some boring grown-up requirement or farming item. Farm tools might arrive wrapped up in brown paper, and day-old chicks were delivered by post in cardboard boxes tied with string, with air-holes in the lid.

Ron and I sent for books of stamps on approval and carefully chose those we wanted for our collections. We were keen on filling in forms and sending off for free samples of whatever was on offer, which would be duly delivered. It could be anything from cough sweets to face cream to knitting wool samples, we didn't care, it was just exciting to receive a package in the post addressed to one of us. I once had the idea of producing a magazine and posting it round to a list of subscribers, whose names I got from a list of competition winners in my *Sunny Stories* comic. Addresses were also supplied, and I wrote to a few and waited hopefully for them to sign up. In the meantime, I produced my first issue, on folded sheets of drawing paper fastened with a staple recycled from another magazine, and filled it with picture strips, text stories, serials with an exciting cliffhanger to grab the interest, quizzes and competitions, all written and illustrated by me. It occurred to me that I would have to do all this every month, a copy for every one of my subscribers, and this was a little daunting. It didn't really matter though, because it didn't catch on, although one boy was kind enough to send back the entry form with a polite refusal.

A telegram was a rare occurrence, usually delivered by someone other than Mr Evans. The war was so fresh in the minds of everyone that a telegram was dreaded as a tiding of bad news, and the sight of that yellow message would bring fear to the heart, even though we had nobody close serving in the forces. The telegraph boys were nicknamed the 'angels of death' during the war and had an unenviable job. Our telegrams, though, would usually indicate no more disastrous news than that a relative was arriving that afternoon, from a certain train or bus, and needed to be met.

CHAPTER TWELVE

The Games We Played

And all about was mine, I said,
The little sparrows overhead,
The little minnows too.
This was the world and I was king;
For me the bees came by to sing,
For me the swallows flew

Robert Louis Stevenson

We were very blessed in having over a hundred acres of farmland as our playground, right outside our back door. We had no need of a playing field or a park. If we wanted a grassy space to play cricket or football or tennis, we could go into a field. If we wanted to climb, there were many varieties and sizes of trees to choose from, or we could climb up walls or on roofs – frowned upon, but we did it anyway. We had a swing on the branch of an apple tree in the orchard. We could make a seesaw from a plank and a log. There were animals to look at if we wanted to. We built houses in trees, dens in bushes, willow huts on marshy ground. We dammed the stream and made stick rafts to sail on them. We never came home from one mealtime to another.

My brother and I had projects that we worked on together, that we didn't divulge to our elders. We built a treehouse in Sunnybank wood, as far away from the house as our land went, hauling wood up to a fork in the branches and nailing it in place with hammer and nails borrowed from the toolbox at home. We hoped that from the ground the leaves would conceal the construction and planned a rope ladder that we could pull up and be unseen. Our dad did not go into that wood very often, and we convinced ourselves no-one knew about the tree house. Probably he knew more than we realised. There were lots of rabbits in Sunnybank; our father went shooting from time to time with his twelve-bore, but it never entered our heads that we might be placing ourselves in the line of fire.

I longed to run away from home and live in the woods, as did children in some of the stories I read, but couldn't quite work out how it could be done. In the stories, children ran away because they had a cruel stepmother or similar; the trouble with that was that none of our elders were cruel at all, they were nice and didn't provide a motive. Finally, I worked out an acceptable solution. Our parents would be called away to look after one or both of our grandparents (they were old, after all) who'd been taken ill, and an unpleasant uncle and aunt would move in to take care of us and the farm for a while. The problem with that was we had no unpleasant aunts and uncles either; what we did have was a very nice granny and aunt already in residence who would have taken good care of us. But these were minor details. We would run away and live in our treehouse. But another problem nagged. We would have to feed ourselves. I had doubts about our ideas of living on nuts and berries and mushrooms, with perhaps the occasional rabbit stew. It sounded okay, but common sense told me we'd need more. So we worked out a scheme. Mr Plunkett the grocer left our weekly supplies in the building just inside our road gate, known as the garage, to be picked up later. If we hid nearby, we could nip out and help ourselves to a few things. After all, we reasoned, we were entitled to our share of the groceries. Needless to say, these elaborate plans came to nought.

Another unrealised runaway option was to live on a desert island; unfortunately our stream had no islands so we created our own by digging trenches and diverting the water to cut off a promising piece of land, preferably with a tree or some bushes on it. They weren't exactly deserted, but they were islands of a sort. We constructed a willow hut on one of them, in a rather damp and boggy patch of ground. We also built fires, illicitly, as we'd been told not to. We cunningly lit them among trees, where we reckoned the smoke would dissipate before it reached above them. We always put them out carefully and scattered the evidence. I think we tried cooking food a few times, not very successfully. We also liked to follow the stream which formed a boundary to part of our land, wading in our wellies, and sometimes came ashore on land that belonged to someone else. We knew we were trespassing but it added to the thrill. If we got near to a farmhouse, usually the Tump, owned by Bill Meredith and his son John, and a dog barked, we'd quickly climb a hedge or squeeze under a fence back into legal territory. We also found it rather exciting to crawl upstream through a water pipe that went under the road near our gate, just big enough in diameter for a child to travel it bent double. We popped up on the other side of the road, where the stream came through the Washpool field. There was always the added thrill that a heavy vehicle passing over might cause the road to collapse when we were in the pipe – it never did.

We did get into serious trouble one time. We'd had the bright idea of running an animal hospital, where we'd doctor up sick or injured wild birds and animals and restore them to health. One of the empty stable stalls could be the hospital ward, and we collected bandages and ointments. The trouble was, we had no patients, so we put up a notice on our road gate, inviting people to bring us their sick and injured. Our dad soon got rid of that. We attempted to treat any of the cats who might seem off-colour; they did not appreciate it and soon discharged themselves from hospital. Then we had a brainwave.

New crops were coming up and, in the fields adjoining Sunnybank, were being nibbled and spoiled by rabbits coming out in the evenings. At that time, rabbits were a huge problem to farmers. Most farms were overrun with them; on any day, especially in the evenings, we could go into a field and find a scene of scores of rabbits hopping about and nibbling at the grass. A loud noise or movement would send them scuttling for their holes with a great bobbing of white tails. They lived in colonies, or 'buries' as they were called, in a bank or under tree roots or near a hedge. Trying to keep their numbers under control was a serious business and one of the reasons that all farmers had shotguns in their homes. Another method of rabbit control was ferreting. My dad had a ferret, a very nasty, vicious yellow-white creature called Joey, who could be handled in safety by no-one but Dad. Ferreting was usually carried out by two or more people together, armed with nets, pegs and the ferret in a bag. Sometimes a terrier went too to sniff out which rabbit holes were occupied. Finding one, the ferret was released into it and a net stretched over the entrance and pegged down securely; when the frightened rabbits came tearing out, often screaming, they came with force and could break through a weak or damaged net. Some ferrets got carried away, and caught and began to eat one of their prey while still underground, and would eventually emerge replete and covered in blood.

This time, the official rabbit catcher had been called in. We never met him, but we immediately hated him and decided he was an enemy. Our sympathies were always with the rabbits, pests or not. A line of gin-traps were set around the perimeter of the wood where foraging rabbits would have to travel. Gin-traps were cruel and vicious devices, their steel jaws snapping shut on any part of an animal that touched them and causing hours of suffering until the captive could be dispatched. Hearing the screams of a trapped animal could make your blood run cold. Thank God they are now illegal. Ron and I formed a rescue committee. The rabbit catcher came early to collect his overnight catch and reset the traps; we would rise even earlier, walk the trapline, release those not much injured, spring the unsprung traps, and take home the injured to our hospital. We'd kill two birds with one stone, so to speak – strike a blow for endangered wildlife and provide our hospital with patients.

We made a few early-morning tours of the trapline, and carried home a few suffering ones, smuggling them into the old stable, where we bandaged wounds and attempted to splint broken limbs. Poor creatures, we must have greatly prolonged their agony. Most died quickly, some lingered for a day or two. We did have one noticeable cure; a rabbit caught by a paw quickly healed, the damaged paw dropped off, and he returned to the wild.

Of course, we were discovered. The rabbit catcher complained to my father of interference with his trapline and his unexpectedly small bag of rabbits; moreover, he had seen prints of small wellie boots in the mud. We were busted. Needless to say, that was the end of Animal Hospital.

Almost all our daylight hours were spent outdoors. We built wigwams out of bean-sticks, made bows and arrows of bendy hazel and practised our archery skills. The one memorable thing about our shooting was that Ron shot a goose, accidentally I'm sure; the goose survived but was injured badly enough to have to be put down. We made Indian headdresses of goose feathers to make our tribal life more authentic and studied Indian life and tradition. If it was wet, we played in the buildings, leaping from the hayloft to a lower level of hay, with a spice of added danger because you never knew whether a stray pikel might have been left behind. We messed about with the loose grain in the granary, strictly forbidden, bringing down wrath on our heads if we were discovered.

Indoor games are not so clear in my memory, maybe because we didn't stay indoors much. I do remember setting up a school for our toys, not just the dolls and stuffed animals, but all the dinky toys, cars and trucks as well. I lined them up in classes and kept a register, a diagonal line in a square for an attendance, a circle for absence. My brother had mechanical toys and I had dolls. I was a tomboy, but I also had a strong maternal streak and I liked my dolls. The first I remember was Elsie, hand-knitted with very long, thin legs. Then there was Ruby, a rather faded nondescript rag doll, and Lucy, with a china head and soft body. Carol was a glamorous blonde with real hair, china-blue eyes that opened and closed and a plaintive voice that said 'Mama'. Her voice failed after a while and she had to be punched to make her speak. Patsy was a doll I was allowed to choose myself from a catalogue; she was billed as a 'realistic baby doll who drinks from her bottle, wets her nappy and can be bathed'. At some point Patsy's head was removed by some inquisitive person, revealing to our interested eyes the system of pipes and tubes that kept her innards functioning. I also had a very precious Victorian heirloom doll called Dinah, with a pink-and-white wax face, exquisitely tucked and flounced white underclothes and gown, a straw hat and little kid boots. I was the wrong kind of child to be given a doll like Dinah; my haphazard dealings with her caused her to soon get a less than pristine appearance. So also with my dolls' pram and my miniature working toy sewing machine, both of which soon got a battered and dented look. There was Rosamund, a tiny doll who was my last. The next Christmas I asked for a handbag. I got it, black and shiny, but somehow that year didn't have quite the same thrill.

We had jigsaw puzzles and board games, *Snakes and Ladders* and *Ludo*, and played card games – *Happy Families*, *Snap*, *Strip Jack Naked* and later, *Whist*, which we played with our elders. Auntie taught me to knit, laboriously in garter stitch with big needles. She was a great knitter, following intricate patterns, fair-isle, cable, fancy stitches for jumpers, cardigans, gloves, hats, scarves. She knitted colourful fair-isle berets which, if we happened to be caught in a rainstorm, had to be dried stretched over a plate to prevent shrinkage. My mother knitted too, but she had little patience for fancy stuff and mostly stuck to socks, knitting them of hard-wearing Welsh wool on four shiny steel needles, requiring great concentration when a heel was to be turned. I learned to be a good knitter but never mastered four needles. I learned to sew a little.

On winter evenings we sat around the kitchen table, adults and children, playing word games, spelling games, card games. Ron and I collected things; stamps which we sent away for, choosing what we could afford from books of 'approvals' and sticking them into albums with transparent hinges, learning a lot of geography in the process. I collected wildflowers, pressing them between sheets of blotting paper in a large heavy book. I'm afraid we also collected birds' eggs, which was legal then, though we never took more than one from a nest and never more than one of each species. The eggs had to be blown, a delicate operation from a pinhole at each end of the egg. Also, to my shame, we dabbled with collecting butterflies, though we never had the required poison pot for killing them and had to wait until one died. I don't think that lasted long, thankfully.

Pets were an important part of our lives. Surrounded by farm animals, a sheepdog and numerous cats, we wanted 'real' pets. Nip was a working dog who was mostly confined to the Engine House. His claim to fame was that whenever the fire station siren went off down the valley, he would wait for it to die away and then give an impressive repeat performance at just the right pitch. We had cats galore; all farms needed them for rat and mice control. Some were half-feral, others petted and more friendly. A notable house-cat in my infancy was called Princess.

But we longed for the kind of pets that we read about in books, a non-working dog or, for me, a pony. I never got the pony and was resentful about it for a long time. Ron and I kept on the lookout for strays; if a stray dog happened across our paths we would bribe, cajole and induce it to come with us, sometimes helping it along with a string tied to its collar, and then tell our elders it had followed us home and, *please could we keep it?* Sometimes we did, for a day or two, until its rightful owner claimed it. Once we had a beautiful foxhound called Kaiser, who had strayed from the hunt and stayed with us for several days. We also had other people's dogs to lodge with us for a while; there was a boisterous rough-haired terrier called Mick, and we looked after our headmaster's cocker spaniel Blackie while he and his family were on holiday.

When a pet shop opened in Hereford, just round the corner from our bus terminal, it soon became our favourite haunt in the city. We acquired a pair of budgies, mine a beautiful turquoise blue, Ron's green and yellow. Mine was called Jonathan and I tried in vain to teach him to talk. A pair of rabbits soon followed, mine black, Ron's grey, and in due course a series of other small rodents We also had assorted frogs, newts, goldfish, a tortoise, even a slow worm for a time. I preferred the furry pets.

We drew, we painted, we whittled things out of pieces of wood, Ron made Airfix models, I wrote stories. Once, we embarked on a mushroom-growing enterprise; we saw an advert that guaranteed a large financial return if we purchased from their firm the necessary starter kit. We bought the kit, we followed the instructions, but alas, we never grew so much as a single button.

Mostly though, we read.

CHAPTER THIRTEEN

The Books We Read

Here's an adventure! What awaits
Beyond those closed mysterious gates?
Whom shall I meet, where shall I go?
Beyond the lovely land I know?
Above the sky, across the sea
What shall I learn, and feel, and see?
Open, strange doors, for good or ill!
I hold my breath a moment still
Before the magic of your look.
What shall you do to me, O book?

Anon.

There did not seem to be, that I remember, many books for very young children in our house, although there were plenty of grown-up volumes. I do remember a few picture-books; *The Billy and Bunny Book*, a pictorial *House that Jack Built*, a simplified, illustrated version of *Where the Rainbow Ends*. I have dim memories of learning to read, of the excitement of finding that the black marks on paper had sounds and could be fitted together to make words, and that the words told a story!

Once I could read, I devoured books as fast as I could get my hands on them, whether suitable for my age or not. I had classics that had belonged to the adults in the household; *Treasure Island*, *The Wind in the Willows*, *Alice in Wonderland*, the *Katy* books, *Little Women* and others. My mother had a lot of books inherited from deceased relatives, many of them had a particularly Victorian flavour, moralistic and preachy and meant to be improving to the reader. I read them all. There was one called *Nat the Naturalist* which particularly grabbed my imagination. My paternal grandmother gave me a book of *Russian Fairy Tales*, lurid and scary, which I devoured with a kind of horrified fascination – though they were no worse, I suppose, than Grimm's and

Andersen's fairy tales, of which we also had copies. She also gave me *A Princess of Servia* (Serbia) which I read and re-read and which made me wonder whether my wandering grandfather ever had any contact with Baltic countries. Among my mother's books was one called *Laddie*, by Gene Stratton-Porter. I loved that book, for the portrayal of life in a large family and for its vivid background of the natural world. I also fell in love with the setting of rural Indiana, and have loved the vast and varied North American continent ever since, helped along by Mark Twain, L.M. Alcott, L.M. Montgomery, Jack London, and later, Madeleine L'Engle and Laura Ingalls Wilder.

And then there were the library books. A library opened in Hay-on-Wye during my childhood and my family fell on it like hungry wolves. People were allowed, I think, up to four books per week, which, with four adults in the house, could amount to sixteen. I'm not sure whether Granny took out books; Auntie certainly did. There was no children's section at that time, though one came along a few years later. Consequently, we children seized upon and read the adult books, discovering such authors as A. Conan Doyle, Somerset Maugham, J. Rider Haggard, H.E. Bates and many, many others. My father liked adventure books, and he was also a great fan of Ralph Whitlock and A.G. Street, both of them farmers who had had humble beginnings and had become famous for their books and radio broadcasts. He had a collection of A.G. Street's novels, which I later read and found to be wonderfully evocative of the rural life. *Farmers Glory*, *The Endless Furrow* and *Strawberry Roan* are three titles that spring to mind – there were many more. There was a radio programme called *Cowleaze Farm*, presented by Ralph Whitlock, which we all listened to; Ralph Whitlock had a wonderfully rich rolling Dorset accent and a relaxed manner. Mum and Auntie preferred family dramas. I did not always understand what I was reading, but it didn't matter. My father, however, decided that not everything was suitable for our young minds, so took it upon himself to censor the books, sometimes advising my mother, 'Better not let the kids read this one.'

My reaction was to get hold of the book and find what the fuss was about – sometimes not a lot that I could see, though there were some steamy sex scenes that probably added to my education. Mostly, though, I liked the adventure books; *King Solomon's Mines*, *The Call of the Wild*, *The White Company*. Of course, we all read the Sherlock Holmes books and discussed them, as Sir Arthur Conan Doyle had supposedly written

The Hound of the Baskervilles in our village, giving his name to the Baskerville Arms.

I read indoors and out, up a tree, in the barns, in the garden. Once I lost a favourite book in the hay barn; it never came to light, but decades later I found a copy of it in the Railway Bookshop in Alnwick, Northumberland. We read in the evenings by the light of an oil lamp in the kitchen, we read by flickering candlelight in bed. It's a wonder that we never (a) got severe eyestrain, or (b) burned the house down. Apart from the odd bit of singed hair from getting too close to the candle, we never set fire to anything. Reading by candlelight had other problems; tilting candlesticks to get a better light would sometimes drip hot wax on to the book covers and sometimes the pages. The books went back to the library on Thursdays; my mother would spend most of Wednesday evening removing blobs of hard candle wax from the library books.

I did not get into the popular children's books of the time until much later. Enid Blyton was a name that popped up in school; my friends liked to compare notes and compete to be the one with the most Enid Blytons. Always eager to be in with the crowd, I requested Enid Blyton books. The first I owned was the *Mystery of the Disappearing Cat*, bought for me when I had my tonsils out. Then I read *Five Go Off in a Caravan*, and I was hooked, and from thence forward gathered my own collection. Enid Blyton as a writer was a strange phenomenon. Her young heroes and heroines seemed to have just one characteristic each – Julian the leader, Dick the second-in-command, George the girl-in-shorts-who-wants-to-be-a-boy, Anne the girly-girl in a dress. The adventures usually had adult criminals in them whom the children outwitted every time, and the baddies were invariably nasty people. The characters were middle-class to the point of snobbishness; the mothers had cooks and maids, the children went to boarding schools except when they were on their hols. Yet the adventures were gripping, fast-moving, and full of danger and excitement and a freedom not known to the children of today. Enid Blyton did a great service to literature because she got children reading.

We had magazines at home too, or 'comics' as they were known. My first was *Sunny Stories*, also written by Enid Blyton (though that meant nothing to me at the time); my brother had a *Mickey Mouse* comic. Later we graduated to *School Friend* and *Lion* respectively, which we took for years and years. I loved *School Friend;* it had a variety of settings to the stories which stimulated the imagination. I longed to be cast away on a desert island like *Jill Crusoe*, or travel West in a Conestoga wagon like the *Children of the Wyoming Trail*. There was still a bit of snobbishness though; all the school stories were set in boarding schools, some in glamorous locations like a chalet school in Switzerland, or a riding-based school or ballet school, and made one's own life and school seem very humdrum. I got the *School Friend Annual* at Christmas for years, still have some of them, but somehow they never quite matched up to the weekly comics with their cliffhangers. I read boys' comics too, especially the ones that featured text stories with thrilling heroes, *Victor*, *Rover*, *Hotspur*, *Wizard*. And, of course, the much-loved *Beano* and *Dandy*.

There were adult periodicals too; the *Farmer and Stockbreeder*, the *Farmer's Weekly*, the local newspapers, the occasional women's magazines that Mum or Auntie bought – *Woman's World*, *Woman's Weekly* (especially popular for the knitting patterns), gardening magazines, *Ladies' Home Journal*, *People's Friend*. Granny had her *Christian Herald*, which she passed on to me when she had finished. We had sets of encyclopaedias – an old but fascinating green-covered set with topics arranged in alphabetical order, interspersed with an interesting picture serial called *Tales the Woodman Told*. At some point my mother was persuaded by a travelling salesman to buy a modern up-to-date set of ten, *Cassell's Children's Book of Knowledge*, which we adored and read almost from cover to cover. I believe the set cost ten guineas, a big sum in those days, although I think it could be paid in instalments. Each of the ten books had a different theme – *The Natural World*, *Feats of Engineering*, *Literature and Poetry*, etc. We learned a lot from those encyclopaedias. It was money well spent.

Strangely, there were well-known authors that I did not discover until later in life: Arthur Ransome, Madeleine L'Engle, C.S. Lewis, Tolkien and others. I started on Dickens as a child and discovered more of his books as I grew. Shakespeare came in fits and starts but I grew to love his language and his plots.

I haven't mentioned poetry, but that played a huge part in my early life. My mother and aunt had been taught poetry by rote, reams of it, and could recite, word-perfect, an epic saga at the drop of a hat. They would often go about their daily tasks declaiming long passages of verse, and many bedtimes, in the room I shared with Auntie, I would watch her brush out her waist-length hair and beg her to recite a poem. She delivered them dramatically with much passion and I would hold my breath as the saga unfolded. The only complaint I had was the invariably tragic endings; I can think of very few that ended happily. There was

Lucy Grey, the little girl who sank into a bog taking lunch to her father; Lord Ullin's daughter, who drowned with her lover; the *Wreck of the Hesperus*, where the skipper's little daughter with 'eyes as blue as the fairy flax, her cheeks like the dawn of day, her bosom white as the hawthorn buds that ope in the month of May' perished in a terrible storm, frozen stiff and lashed to the ship's mast. The *Mistletoe Bough* told of a bride having a playful game of hide-and-seek with her new husband, hiding in an oak chest and someone finding decades later that 'a skeleton form lay mouldering there, in the bridal dress of that lady fair'. What pathos! Such tragedy! A few were more uplifting sagas of heroism – there was Barbara Freitchie, who boldly defied the confederate army and flew the union flag, winning the respect of Stonewall Jackson himself.

> *'Who touches a hair of that old grey head*
> *Dies like a dog! March on!' he said.*

And Horatius, who 'kept the bridge' against the hordes of Tuscany.

My aunt had a volume of Longfellow's poems, bound in leather and much admired by me. It had been given to her on her twelfth birthday by her mother. She let me read it, and I fell in love with the long narrative poems; *The Courtship of Miles Standish*, *Evangeline*, and *The Ride of Paul Revere*, redolent of different times in American history. Most of all, I loved the lilting cadence of *The Song of Hiawatha* and read it so many times that I knew some parts of it by heart. It conjured up for me the world of the Native American to a T. To my delight, Auntie promised me she'd pass on the book to me on my twelfth birthday and she was true to her word. I have it still, the leather a bit scuffed, the book a bit shabby and the print now looking impossibly small, but all down the years it's been well read and well loved.

Some of the books I read as a child held a kind of magic, impossible to describe and re-create. There was *Mossy Green Theatre*, *Widgery Winks in the Wide World*, *Bevis*, the story of a boy. Reading *Bevis* as an adult I disliked it; Bevis seemed a very snobbish and domineering boy, ordering his friends about and given to beating his dog. Such is the difference between adult perspective and looking at things through the eyes of childhood.

CHAPTER FOURTEEN

High Days and Holidays

*People don't notice whether it's winter or summer when
they're happy.*

Anton Chekov

Our days had their routines, and so did our weeks, our months and
our years. Thursday was set apart as market day, for my mother
and for us children when we were not at school. At 10.20 precisely,
having washed us, dressed us in our best, attended to her own toilette,
which included her best coat or costume or dress, court shoes and
stockings, collected her various bags and baskets of goods for sale and
walked the rough track across two fields, my mother would be waiting
at the road gate for the market bus. This motor, owned by Sargeants of
Kington, would travel from the terminal to Hay and back every
Thursday, picking up farmers' wives and families, and sometimes the
farmers themselves all along the way. We would hear it coming from a
distance with its familiar droning, the grinding of gears as they were
changed, and finally its appearance round the corner and down the hill
to stop at our gate.

The bus would be already almost full, with farmers' wives with their
infants and baskets of produce, which varied according to the time of
year. There might be butter if there was a surplus, dressed chickens or
ducks, fruit in season if there happened to be a glut, even little bunches
of snowdrops, arranged attractively with a bit of evergreen, which the
dealers coming from the Welsh valleys snapped up like hot cakes. Eggs
were usually collected from home by the 'egg-man', in wooden crates
with the eggs stacked snugly in layers in cardboard trays. The market bus
was a great place to catch up with the gossip of the past week. Tongues
would clack and there would be a buzz of voices and laughter as we
lumbered on our way, stopping at various lane ends and farm gates to
pick up more passengers. We would travel through Clyro and the last
mile up the hill known as Longlands and then down into Hay, over the

river bridge and finally come to rest by the town clock, where the bus would disgorge its load.

There'd be three hours before we had to begin our return journey. My mother's first task would be to deliver her produce to the traders whose stalls lined Broad Street. Then we'd go about the business of the day. There was the Limited for household items, Gwilym's for haberdashery and knitting wool, Grant's for our bundle of weekly papers and magazines. The Street (market) had to be browsed. We needed to visit Mr Plunkett the grocer with our shopping list for Saturday delivery. Maybe Miss Nellie Lewis the butcher in Broad Street or Tony Pugh the fishmonger in Lion Street. We'd change the library books. If there was clothing to be purchased, we'd visit Golesworthy's (where the staff knew all the customers and their families, and where our feet were always carefully measured for shoes and our growth remarked upon). There was Jones the tailor next door, or Trevor Pugh on the corner of Lion Street for men's requirements, or Briggs and Miss Deeson's for the ladies. We were allowed to take several garments at a time home on trial, the ones that did not suit to be returned the next week. I remember agonising over three summer dresses when I was a little older. As an extra treat, we might get sweets or an ice-cream cornet from Pughs the Pavement, where Mr and Mrs Pugh had shelves full of brightly-coloured jars of sweeties which they weighed out by the quarter pound. And we'd be sure to meet up with one of my aunties and go for a cup of tea and plate of cakes at the Wye Café or the Snack Bar in Castle Street. If we didn't consume all the cakes on the spot, we'd be given a doggy bag to take the rest home. Laden down with our purchases, we'd catch the bus home, stocked up with goods and gossip for another week.

My mother kept detailed account of her spending, down to the last halfpenny. Some of her accounts for early 1945 read as follows (not all purchased in the same week!)

> *Grocery: 9 shillings 11½ pence (just under 50p in today's currency)*
> *Oranges: 3s 9d*
> *Axe handle: 2s 2d*
> *Bread (two weeks): 7s 2d*
> *Overalls: 10s 7d*
> *Stamps: 3s 4d*
> *Sweets: 1s 0d*

Soap: 2s 10d
Wool: 5s 0d
Bus: 1s 2d
2 shirts: 17s 0d
Boots(self): £1. 1s. 6d
Salt: 3s 4d
Jacket (Baden): £1. 13s. 0d
Shoes (Eleanor): 10s 6d
Tea: 1s 6d
Papers: 8d
18 chicks: 18s 0d (bought at a day old and delivered by post)
Matches: 1½d
Shoe repairs: 3s 4d
Shoes (Ron): 10s 6d
2 pairs Wellingtons: £1. 5s. 2d
Screws: 10d
Repairs to binder: 10s 0d
Meat: 4s 6d
Stockman's coat: 15s 6d
Hen house: £12. 00
Doctor's bill: £3. 15s. 6d
Eye ointment: 7½d
Trousers (Baden): £1. 1s. 9d
Petrol: 3s 10d
Milk of magnesia: 2s 10d
Coat (self): £5. 5s. 0d

She must have been saving her clothing coupons for a while to get that last purchase!

Sunday had a routine of its own too, and meant Sunday dinner, church, a fire in the parlour, a relaxed feel to the day.

Once every few months we might take a trip to Hereford, which meant commissioning Bill Powell's taxi to take us to Clyro and/or bring us back, then picking up the Midland Red bus which passed through the village. We would alight at the Horse and Groom pub in Eign Street at the edge of the city, and our first stop would usually be Westwoods' Fish and Chip shop just along the street, where we would enjoy cod and chips with bread and butter and a cup of tea. The pet shop, when it opened, was in the same area and we would have to nip in there to see what was new, or to order birdseed or rabbit pellets to be picked up on our way home, with the hope that we might pick up a new pet as well. Then we would venture into the city centre. Hereford, with its historic black-and-white buildings was, and is, an interesting city, but my favourite destination was Woolworths, where I would spend whatever money I had on stationery, taking ages to choose just the right exercise books, rubbers, pencils, paper clips and folders. I just loved stationery. Ballpoint pens, known then as Biros, were not in common use and I looked longingly at the expensive fountain pens. When I received one for a birthday one year, I was overjoyed. I cherished that pen, a Platignum, in its own little padded case, and kept it for years.

Occasionally we were taken to absorb some culture as well as shop. I remember visiting the cathedral and the museum, and there were probably other places.

Easter Saturday was the time for a visit to Glasbury, where my mother's family – her parents, uncles, aunts and her sister Edie – were buried in the graveyard on a bank overlooking the road at St. Peter's Church. My mother would trim the grass, tidy up and arrange fresh flowers, usually primroses and daffodils, while we kids amused ourselves looking at the names on gravestones. Mother's Aunt Gladys (known as Gladdie, to distinguish her from numerous other ladies named Gladys in the family) lived in a gracious villa called Melbourne, next door to the church where her late husband had once been the vicar. Part of the Easter ritual was tea at Melbourne after the graveyard visit. Aunt Gladdie had been a teacher, was small and sprightly and bird-like; her home was always spotlessly shining and polished and in perfect order, unlike the casual living we enjoyed at home. We had a dainty tea on her gleaming round table and had to mind our manners or we would 'cop it' from our mother later. After tea, there would be a visit to Auntie Gladdie's sister, Auntie Bessie, who lived at the Tram Road, a house further up the hill and reached by a short walk up Aunt Gladdie's sloping garden. Aunt Bessie was a heartier, jollier version of her sister and seeming more down-to-earth and less genteel, maybe because she had a large family of children and Auntie G. had none. Her family had branched out in all kinds of interesting directions. Her youngest daughter, Roma, was a midwife and was in attendance when I gave birth to my first child. Auntie Bessie's husband, Uncle Arthur, was a portly man and, I think, disabled in some way; he would sit most of the day in the glass porch at the front of the house, leaning on his walking stick and looking down over the garden and the valley.

For several years, until their deaths, we also visited another cottage on the Green in Glasbury, where lived Aunt Margaret and her sister Aunt Cilla, who were great-aunts of my mother and were very old; one of them lived to be almost a hundred. I liked going there; they had lots of books and often gave us one each to take home, and sometimes a shilling for each of us as well, a lot of money in those days.

Hay Fair was an event that happened twice a year, in May and November. Then the town would be magically transformed with bright lights, roaring machines, loud blaring music and glittering movement. Rides and swings and dodgem cars and sideshows would fill the upper part of Oxford Road, making it look strange and unfamiliar and full of colour. When we were small, we had sedate rides on little horses that gently moved up and down and round and round. The more exciting rides came later, with girlfriends and, if you were lucky, a few boys you fancied. The fair was a great place for budding teenage romance.

We went on day trips to the seaside, at least one every year, a school or church trip, to Porthcawl, or Barry or Swansea or Tenby. We played in the sand or paddled in the sea, the girls with their dresses tucked into their knickers. The seaside visit I remember most vividly was to Aberystwyth, when we were no more than toddlers and the war had not yet come to an end. It stands out for me because my dad came too, a rare happening. I don't remember one family holiday we had when we were all together. Farmers didn't take holidays. But he came that day. We played on the beach with our shiny new buckets and spades. But suddenly there was a commotion. Two roaring mechanical monsters came charging down the beach and plunged into the sea. My parents called them ducks, which puzzled me, because they were nothing like our ducks at home. Years later, when I saw amphibian ducks close up, I was surprised at how small they were. The ones at Aberystwyth had seemed huge and very scary.

On the way home we stopped at Devil's Bridge and went to see the falls. I don't remember the water; my memory is of my dad carrying me down what seemed endless flights of steep stone steps. He held me so tight that my leg was being pinched, but I felt safe. I always did when my dad carried me, or held me in front of him on one of the carthorses, or sat me on his knee at home.

Summer meant holidays, and we children had them even if our parents didn't. There were two holiday destinations. One was to our Auntie Mary's near Llyswen. She had moved from my birthplace on the Begwyns and now lived at a farm called Lower Rhydness. It was only about seven miles away, we were going from one farm to another, but there were differences. My aunt and uncle's house was bigger and posher than ours; it had interesting nooks and crannies and passageways and, the height of luxury to us, electricity and a proper bathroom with hot and cold running water! It was there that we learned to ride bikes, guided and supported by our older girl cousins Doreen and Margaret, up and down their winding farm drive.

The other holiday destination was much more of an adventure because our mum came too and it took a whole day's travelling to get there. Our paternal grandparents had settled at Longlands farm near Whitbourne on the Hereford/Worcester border, farming the rich red cider-growing, beef-producing soil. The rift between my parents and grandparents had been healed, chiefly, I think, due to my mother's efforts; it was she who came with us on our visits. It was always tacitly understood that my father couldn't leave the farm, which of course was true. I am so glad they made up their differences. Our lives were enriched by our visits to Longlands and we would have missed out on so much.

Today it would be a couple of hours' drive away at the most. It took us a whole day of travelling. First, Mr Powell's car to Clyro, then a bus to Hereford, where we changed at the bus terminal and waited for the appropriate bus bound for Worcester. This dropped us off at the roadside at the end of the long drive leading to our grandparents' farm. Sometimes we would be met by Uncle Archie's car, but if he was busy, we had to trudge the long, meandering road, carrying our cases, until the farm came in sight. The farmhouse was an impressive one, mellow red brick with tall chimneys and an L-shaped wing, approached by a pretty bridge over a wide stretch of water. We loved the house and grounds. It had no mod cons at all, no electricity and the water was pumped from a well in the yard. There were attics, cellars, a kitchen where most of the daily living went on, other rooms accessed by dim hallways and mysterious doors. One door was kept locked and must never be entered; we were told that the floor of the cupboard inside was rotten and could plunge you down to the cellars below, which gave us a delicious thrill every time we passed on our way to bed. Grandad had ships in bottles, all with fascinating detail, and other interesting objects on his desk. One wing upstairs was mostly unused but had rooms that were large, light and airy, empty except for a covering of straw, where apples were stored for the winter. My granny's housekeeping skills were limited because of her disability, and the whole house had an air of slight neglect, which only added to the charm. Outside at the back was a walled courtyard, which led to a shrubbery full of unusual plants and evergreens. The farm was part of the Whitbourne Hall estate, owned by Captain Evans, the heir of a vinegar-making baron, who had travelled the world and brought back many tropical and exotic trees and shrubs to the estate. We loved finding the unusual cones and seed heads from the trees. A road led past Longlands to the Hall; we had the run of the farm but anywhere past the big gates was forbidden and we could only gaze through the gates. The Hall itself, built in neo-Palladian style in the nineteenth century by the Evans family, was very beautiful, its pillared structure standing out as a landmark in the area. We loved the wildlife at Longlands, especially the waterfowl on the big ponds, which were stocked with fish, coots and ducks and moorhens, and the kingfishers and water voles that we saw if we watched quietly. Grandad had been a gamekeeper and had something of a fearsome reputation; with us he was gruff but kind. Granny loved us dearly and Uncle Archie was always kind. We loved our visits there and went home laden down with fruit, produce, books and at least once with a kitten in a box, which escaped on the bus and caused a degree of havoc. Longlands was a big part of our childhood.

We had modest celebrations at Hallowe'en and November 5th, carving out turnip heads and putting candles inside, and maybe a few times we tried bobbing for apples, or attempted to make toffee apples. On Guy Fawkes night we had a bonfire, complete with guy wearing old Wellingtons with holes, and a modest firework display – Catherine wheels, jacky-jumpers, bangers, a rocket or two. The main thing I remember about November 5th is that it was invariably wet and muddy.

Christmas was something we looked forward to with great anticipation, but before we could enjoy it, we had to suffer the ordeal of the annual slaughter of geese for Christmas dinners, a major source of income for most farmers and their wives. This took place a week or so before the 25th. For several days the place would be a charnel house of dead geese, plucked geese, dressed geese and *feathers!* The whole process was called feathering and it was an apt description. Everyone helped, sitting round the kitchen fire draped in coarse aprons, with a dead goose, to be plucked while still warm, across our laps; even my dad and us children, as soon as our little fingers could pull out the breast feathers, the easiest to pluck. My father did the slaughtering, up before daybreak, although my mother had no qualms herself about dispatching poultry (and it wasn't done in the most humane way in those days); she would have her work cut out getting ready for the marathon of feathering and dressing. There were buckets for the feathers; my mother saved them for pillows and feather beds, and you had to watch that the dead goose across your lap didn't drip blood into the feather bucket. She saved the wings too, sometimes using them in the old-fashioned way for sweeping the hearth. The feathers and fluff couldn't be contained, but floated off everywhere, upstairs and down, in every nook and cranny, settling in one's hair and getting up one's nose. The warm, greasy smell of numbers of dressed geese was not nice, and we had a fire going in the parlour so we could eat meals there away from it all. It was a miserable time, and I would wonder however we could have a nice Christmas after suffering it.

But miraculously, we always did. By the time the day came, the geese would be away to their destinations of someone's Christmas dinner table. During the war years, geese were often sold on the 'black market' – I have memories of dark evenings when a van would come, without headlights, to pick up a load of contraband.

The house would somehow be swept clear of feathers and unpleasant odours, the furniture would be polished, paper chains made and hung up, a Christmas tree installed and all would be ready. Getting to sleep on Christmas Eve was difficult. Having hung up our grey woollen stockings on the ends of the beds, we tried to sleep to make the morning come more quickly. Always an anxious child, I worried that Father Christmas would come before I was asleep and go away again, or that I wouldn't sleep at all and he wouldn't come at all... Needless to say, I always went to sleep and he always delivered. When we woke, the limp grey stockings would be bursting with exciting bulges and lumps and things that crackled when we touched them. Often in the early hours we unpacked them and looked at the modest contents – an orange, sugar mouse, chocolate coins, maybe a small toy or two, a comic and a cracker sticking out of the top. There would be our 'big' present beside the bed, and a book. We usually examined everything, read some of our new books, ate some chocolate and went back to sleep.

The day would bring carols on the radio, with my mother warbling along, the smell of Christmas dinner in the oven, eating more chocolate,

Christmas cake, mince pies and crackers at tea time, a blazing fire, maybe playing any new games we might have, trying out new toys. The outside work had to be done, cows milked, animals fed, but the adults spent most of the day indoors with us. It was simple, but it was a special time, and we loved it.

CHAPTER FIFTEEN

Entertainment

*I find television very entertaining. Every time somebody turns
on the set, I go into the other room and read a book.*

Groucho Marx

We did not expect to be entertained, and mostly, we made our own entertainment. Reading came top of the list for most of the people in our household. There were the library books, our own collection of assorted literature gathered over the years, a good part from past generations. There were the weekly comics and magazines, the *Brecon and Radnor Express* and *The Hereford Times*. The bookshelves in our house were stuffed full to overflowing.

Television was becoming popular, but it was out of reach for us because it would be another decade or more until the power lines reached us and brought the wonders of electricity. There were a few special visits to fortunate people who already had TV sets, strictly educational programmes like the *Trooping of the Colour* or the *Ascent of Everest*. The screens were small, grainy, black and white flickering pictures and terse, clipped commentaries, but a thing of wonder to the likes of us. We were invited to the home in Hay of our mother's cousin Tom to watch the magic box, or occasionally a favoured few of Mr Evans' class would go next door to watch some current affairs programme that would improve our minds and broaden our outlooks.

But we did have the radio, or, as it was known then, the 'wireless' – box-shaped Bakelite on a stand that revolved to catch the best signal and was a vital part of our equipment for keeping up with national and international news, for information and for entertainment. The wireless had knobs to find the right station (*The Light Programme* and the *Home Service* were the two most used) and for controlling volume. Much twiddling of the knobs was usually needed to get it right. We children also got ticked off fairly frequently for twirling the wireless around fast to hear the amusing squeaks and squawks of voices cutting in and out.

Dinner was at 1pm, and my dad would be there on the dot to listen the news and, of equal importance, the weather forecast. He then usually gave his views on the current national and political situation during the meal and what in his opinion should be done about it all. My parents were staunch Tories; when once, in a burst of childish altruism, I gave my view that those who had a lot of money should share it with those who hadn't, my parents looked horrified and my mother exclaimed, 'But that's socialist kind of talk!'

At 1.45 came *Listen With Mother*, a soothing programme of familiar nursery rhymes and gentle stories for small children, followed by *Women's Hour*, which my mother listened to if she happened to be in the house. My mother spent minimal time indoors, much preferring to be out in the open air, working in her garden or helping my dad or organising her poultry world. She adored her garden, had the greenest of green fingers, and could coax growth from any seed or cutting or root. When she began to travel abroad in later years, she took cuttings and seed pods from anything she fancied and suffered agonies of guilt and fear going through customs. She once told me that if she'd had the chance, she would have studied botany, and in particular, trees. We children had our own little garden patches, in which we hopefully planted seeds and watched for growth. I had a gooseberry bush in mine.

It was Auntie, I think, who was the more house-proud one, polishing furniture, rubbing up brasses until they gleamed, ironing and folding laundry. It was she who periodically flung out all the upstairs rugs and beat them to within an inch of their lives with a wicker carpet beater, who swept and dusted and applied Mansion polish and Brasso. Maybe it was Auntie who was the one I listened to afternoon radio with most often while she did the ironing with old-fashioned flat-irons that had to be heated on the range and clipped into a metal cover. The talks and interviews on *Women's Hour* I mostly found boring and over my head, but I did enjoy the fifteen-minute serialisation of a novel read at the end. I remember *Adam Bede* read in the unforgettable voice of Gladys Young, and *The Moonstone*, and *Brat Farrar*, although the readers of those have escaped me. Five o'clock brought tea-time and *Children's Hour*, introduced by Uncle Mac (Derek McCullough, who also played the part of Larry the Lamb in the ongoing saga of Toytown, along with the other characters: Dennis the Dachshund, who spoke with a strong German accent, placing his verbs at the end of a sentence; Ernest the Policeman; grumpy Mr Grouser; the Inventor; and the Mayor and others. There were other entertaining programmes on *Children's Hour*, the Jennings stories, *Out With Romany*, *Nature Parliament*, *Sherlock Holmes*, *Worzel Gummidge* and many others. Uncle Mac always ended the programme with 'Goodnight children – everywhere.'

After *Children's Hour* came the six o'clock news, followed by the weather forecast and then the shipping forecast, the stations being forever imprinted on my memory because of the fascinating names: Bailey, Fisher, Fastnet, German Bight, Rockall, Malin, North and South Utsire, Cromarty, Forth, and so on and so on. At 6.45 came the eagerly awaited latest episode in the thrilling adventure serial *'Dick Barton, Special Agent'*. Just hearing the rousing fast-paced signature tune, the *Devil's Gallop*, would send shivers of delighted apprehension down my spine. Dick Barton invariably came out on top through all the dangers, with his two mates Snowy and Jock, but the serial always ended with a tantalising cliff-hanger, leaving us tense with suspense until the next evening. We were gutted when the series ended, to be replaced by *The Archers*, an everyday story of country folk, with whom we could identify but whose rather humdrum lives held little thrill. I was doubly disappointed because I thought *The Archers* was going to be about Robin Hood.

Seven o'clock saw the start of the evening programmes. There was something to look forward to most evenings. There were quiz shows, like *Top of the Form*, with competing schools. There were comedies – *Educating Archie*, *Life With the Lyons*, *Much Binding in the Marsh*, *Ray's a Laugh*. There was Wilfred Pickles with *Have a Go*. Another detective serial was *Paul Temple Investigates*, which was also introduced by rousing, fast-moving music, the *Coronation Scott*. And then there was *Journey into Space*, which surely must have been the most exciting of them all, when we were no longer earthbound but transported into the world of Jet Harris and his three sidekicks, Lemmy, Mitch and Doc. The exploration of space was becoming a real possibility, and we felt that we were on the cusp of things undreamed of, and that one day space travel would no longer be something in the realm of fantasy fiction.

Occasionally, when we were a little older, we were allowed to stay up and listen to grown-up programmes, notably once or twice when I listened to *Saturday Night Theatre*, which ended very late indeed on a Saturday night. One was a dramatization of *Lord of the Flies*, which struck terror into my heart and probably gave me nightmares for a long time. The real horror of it was that this was no fantasy story, but one about an ordinary group of boys left alone without adult supervision. It sent my vivid imagination into overdrive once more.

There were occasional events that we attended in the village, a 'social' now and then, a concert or a visit to the pantomime. We'd have coach trips to the seaside in summer, or special events to celebrate some momentous occasion, like the Coronation. We went to tea with various relatives, or they came to tea with us.

Neighbours were very important to farming families in the days without phone, Internet, or even a car in our young days. My father eventually got a Land Rover but I was well into my teens by then. Our neighbours were the first people we turned to in time of trouble, to advise, assist, share, lend or borrow whatever happened to be the need of the moment. You could depend on them. In between times of need, we visited to pass the time of day, or because we hadn't visited for a while, or maybe to share some fruit or veg if there was a surplus, or to take a bunch of flowers from our garden. And naturally, to keep up with the latest news or gossip. We walked of course, across fields, over stiles, through gates that had to be carefully closed behind us. We children enjoyed visiting; usually it would be the elder members of the household who would entertain us, the younger ones being busy at work, and they always made a fuss of us. Mrs Lloyd, Pen-y-cae lived just above us with her bachelor son Tom, a red-faced jolly John Bull of a man, who always came to help at threshing time or pig killing. Mrs Lloyd was a jolly lady too, with round rosy cheeks, her hair in a bun, and a long white apron. She seemed to be always baking, and we had little cakes fresh from the oven when we went there. In the other direction, down the road, at Crossway, lived Mrs Harris and her son Trevor, who was something of an engineer and operated the threshing machine. Trevor was a popular, kind, smiley man who loved children. Later his mother remarried and moved into town. Trevor married Joan, a former nurse from Birmingham, who settled well into country life and became firm friends with our family, cemented by the fact that their two daughters, Carol and Jenny, were around the age of our younger brother Tim. A little further down the road and round the bend, a lane to the left led to Crossfoot, the home of Mr and Mrs Tom Watkins. They were a childless couple with a big house and Mrs Watkins was rather more house-proud than most farm wives. I remember highly polished furniture and lace doyleys and delicate china teacups. She was always pleased to see us and struck up a particular friendship with Auntie.

But the visits we enjoyed most of all were to Bythel, home of the three elderly Price siblings and their nephew Fred. The Prices had previously rented the farm we now lived in and had moved to a smaller place when, I suppose, it got too much for them. John was the oldest, a portly bespectacled man who smoked a pipe and wore a waistcoat with a pocket watch and chain. When I later saw pictures of Arthur Ransome and wondered why he seemed strangely familiar, I realised that he reminded me strongly of John Price. John sat in his armchair by the fire puffing on his pipe and did not appear to do any work. Harry and Alice were twins. Harry was the one who did the farm work, a bent, wiry little man who always seemed busy about something or other, carrying sacks or buckets with milk or water and not often sitting down. Alice, his twin, did not resemble him at all; all three seemed completely different. Alice was a quick, lively, apple-cheeked little lady who bustled about between kitchen and dairy and garden, working hard to keep the household going. We adored her; she was almost like another grandmother to us, always plying us with sweets, biscuits or home-made bread, which she baked in a huge old baking oven, always smiling, always cheerful and always pleased to see us. For some reason she never called me by my first name, but by my second, Mary. Fred was their nephew but seemed to my child's eyes to be almost as old as the others. I don't know anything about his parents, or why he lived with his aunt and uncles. He was an eccentric fellow, not much good at farming but a clever and inventive craftsman and engineer. He never rose much before noon, but from our windows we could see the lights in his workshop as he worked into the night. He made two beautiful wooden wagons for Ron and me, painted red and green and filled with building blocks. These lasted through our childhoods, our children's and I believe one of them is still being played with by Ron's grandchildren. There was also a child-size wheelbarrow made by Fred, or maybe we had one each of those too.

The house at Bythel was tiny; as you went in by the front door, another door across the living room led into the garden, and in summer that door would be open, framing a beautiful picture of Alice's garden, ablaze with lupins, delphiniums, hollyhocks, marigolds, stock and sweet-scented blooms of all descriptions, buzzing with bees. We always got a bunch of flowers to take home. So much did we love our visits to Bythel that one day, having been taken there the day before, Ron and I decided we would like to repeat the experience and pay another visit. I was probably three or four, Ron not much more than two and a half. Without more ado we set off, negotiating a field with a fence to get over, under or through; a steep stretch of woodland sloping down to the stream; the stream itself to cross, although I think there were stepping stones; another bank to climb at the other side; which took us to a field and farmyard to cross before we got to the house. Alice must have been surprised to see us, but she was equal to the situation, sitting us down for refreshments while Fred was dispatched to inform our family of our whereabouts.

I continued to visit Alice into my teen years. There must have been a considerable gap between visits at one time, or maybe I'd had a growth spurt, because I now towered over Alice and realised how tiny she was, while she peered up at me and exclaimed, 'Well, Mary, how you've grown!'

Alice had a stroke in the middle of a particularly hard winter when we all found ourselves snowbound; no chance of an ambulance getting there or of any other vehicle to get her the twenty-five miles to the hospital. So as long as the snow lasted, we neighbours took it in turns to nurse her, night and day, and take care of the rest of the household. I stayed one night with my aunt, dozing in the armchair by the fire and going upstairs every hour or so to check on the patient. It was heartbreaking to see her so small and shrunken in the bed, unable to move much and barely conscious, remembering how full of life and vitality and humour she had been. I trudged home through the snow next morning pondering on the brevity and uncertainty of life. Alice went into hospital when the roads cleared, but did not return home and died there a short time later. I do not think she would have been able to settle for a life of disability, dependent on others. I was sixteen or seventeen at the time, and glad I'd been able to share some help and maybe even bring a little bit of comfort to her in her last days.

CHAPTER SIXTEEN

Spring

And the Spring arose on the garden fair,
Like the Spirit of Love felt everywhere:
And each flower and herb on Earth's dark breast
Rose from the dream of its wintry rest.

Percy Bysshe Shelley

pring came late to us, perched as we were on a hillside nine hundred feet above sea level. We searched eagerly for the first signs of the new season, which came before winter quite lost its grip – snowdrops poking up among the dead leaves and sticks and debris of winter, sometimes even before the last of the snow had melted. There was something (and still is, for me) about those brave little green spikes with the white of their bud already showing at their tip, which made my heart rejoice. Nothing deterred them, not even a fresh fall of snow or a hard frost; they kept coming, they multiplied and very soon a nodding white and green sea of them would be there along the hedgerows and under the trees to gladden our hearts. My mother called them 'February Fair Maids' and they were fair indeed to our winter-weary eyes.

Before the snowdrop flowering had ended, there would be daffodils, bold, brave and sturdy, which we hoped would be at their best by Easter for the decoration of family graves. Their appearance usually brought forth a heartfelt rendering of Wordsworth's famous poem from our mother or our aunt, or both.

And then would come the other flowers of spring – blue violets in long grass, primroses along the banks, shiny lacquered celandines and buttercups, delicate wild anemones. Catkins dangled and swung from the hazels, 'lambs' tails' as the older people called them; if you touched them, they left a yellow powder on your fingers. Pale yellow pussy-willow catkins appeared like soft powder puffs. Sticky buds burst on the horse chestnuts, where later we would search for conkers. We found frog spawn in muddy pools and collected it to take home, nurture and watch as small black tadpoles emerged, to later develop little legs and turn into tiny frogs. Some did not survive; we felt it was a supreme achievement to be able to release a little frog or two into the world to fend for itself.

Spring brought the birds out of their winter survival mode into a burst of activity; the dawn chorus greeted each new day as the various species vociferously declared their claim to the most desirable mate or the best nesting site. My brother and I made it our business to locate every nest in the locality and monitor the progress of its inmates. There were the brown and sludgy green speckled eggs of the blackbird, the beautiful azure blue of the song thrush, both in neatly woven and lined nests in a bush or thick hedge, the plain white of the wood pigeon, two eggs on a carelessly flung-together platform of sticks in a bare tree, the tiny white red-splotched robin's egg burrowed into a bank. There were the little blue eggs of the hedge sparrow, the pale ones of the house sparrow. In the meadow below the house, near the boggy patch, the curlews nested, two or more large eggs, greenish splotched for camouflage, laid in not much more than a scoop in the ground, always with the pointed ends facing inwards. Sadly, curlew eggs often came to grief under the wheels of some farm machine. We watched with interest the progress of the nests, consulting bird books to see the length of the incubation time for each, noting with delight a scrap of eggshell on the ground that would indicate hatching, peering in at the ugly, pink, naked little creatures with bulging eyes and insatiable appetites which had emerged. Any movement nearby would signal the possible return with food of the parents, and a mass of eager, wide, demanding yellow beaks would present themselves, attached to wildly flapping little wings and insistent squeaking. We observed how the loudest, most insistent of the brood got fed most often, and therefore grew fastest. We were sad when a pathetic little corpse on the ground showed that one chick had been pushed out of the nest.

While the birds were raising families, my mother's collection of hens, ducks and geese would be doing the same. She watched, eagle-eyed, for signs of broodiness in her hens – an unusual amount of clucking and fussing, a reluctance to move after laying an egg, or indeed, if a hen had come across the eggs of others and had tucked them away under her fluffed-up feathers. Mother set her broody hens in special small coops which they had no inclination to leave, having to be forcibly removed once a day to eat and drink, clucking irritably and not content until they had settled back on their clutch of eggs – twelve or thirteen for hen's eggs, rather less for duck's. Ducks were not considered good mothers, although, having kept ducks in later life, I have found them to be excellent mothers. But in those days, hens were often called in to act as surrogates. Those who had hatched ducklings were comically nonplussed when their nestlings hatched and immediately made for the first puddle of water they could find. Their 'mother' would fuss up and down on the bank, puzzled at the way her babies had turned out.

During the incubation period, the eggs would be tested at intervals to see whether the occupants were alive and well. The eggs would be gently placed in a bucket of lukewarm water, and if all was well, we'd be rewarded by the egg bobbing about as it was kicked from within. If a chick had died, or the egg had turned out to be infertile or addled, it would sink like a stone. We quite enjoyed disposing of the bad eggs by hurling them at the stone wall at the back of one of the buildings, preferably far away from the house because of the smell. When there was a surplus of broody hens, the unwanted ones were banished to a lonely enclosure until they had got over the feeling.

If a particular sitting did not work out according to plan, my mother sometimes supplemented the brood by purchasing day-old chicks, which arrived by post in a cardboard box with airholes punched in the lid, and full of cheeping, bewildered little balls of fluff. Some would have died in transit; there were always a couple of bedraggled corpses among the living. My mother would begin their care by administering a pill to each small chick, pushing it down its throat until it swallowed. What the pill was made of, or what its purpose was, I've forgotten, but there must have been some good reason.

The geese brooded their own eggs and became fiercely protective while doing so. My mother issued dire warnings of what could happen if we were attacked by an irate goose. A blow from a wing or a peck from a hard beak could break the bones of a small child or even prove fatal. The gander was the worst; always bad-tempered and given to sly tweaks from behind, when offspring appeared, he morphed into a murderous psychopath capable of anything. Even my mother carried a stick when dealing with the geese. We kept our distance.

Spring was, of course, lambing time, when for some weeks the concentration of the whole household was focused on the birthing and nurture of the little new creatures. Sheep were not brought inside to lamb in those days, unless there was some particular problem. Several times a day, and throughout the night, someone had the task of 'going round' the ewes, checking and assisting a birth if need be, or reporting back for help if the problem was too great. Ewes had many lambing problems, it seemed; the lamb could be presented head-first (not good, the little hooves and forelegs had to come first for a smooth delivery, followed by the head). They could be lying crosswise, or be extra-large, or it might be a breech presentation or a multiple delivery. Sometimes the womb would prolapse and need to be manually restored. A lot of manoeuvring was done, with someone holding down the suffering mother while someone else worked. A long labour needed help, by grasping the forelegs of the lamb and pulling. I was very proud when I pulled my first lamb, the little creature sliding out in a rush of fluid, shaking its head and struggling to get to its feet almost immediately. The ewe would be immediately flooded with maternal feeling, whickering softly to the newborn and licking it clean.

Most ewes were good mothers. Some, however, failed dismally in one way or another; they gave birth to a dead lamb, or hadn't enough milk for twins, or even downright rejected their young and wandered off. That called for more assistance; a bereaved mother could often be fooled by the skin of her dead lamb being placed over a living one who was motherless or whose mother hadn't enough milk. Sickly or chilled lambs would be taken to the house and rubbed with old sacks in front of the fire to get the blood circulating; sometimes people put them into a warming oven for a while. Milk and brandy would be administered and often the lamb revived and would be returned to its mother. If all else failed, the lambs would be bottle-fed. These 'tiddlers' became something of a pest when they grew bigger, mobbing any human who appeared, bleating and shoving and demanding. Nevertheless, we were fond of them and gave them names. Sadly, they went to market with the rest when the time came.

Spring was also 'turning out' time for cattle kept inside through the winter, usually when the grass had begun to grow again. The sight of newly liberated cattle was something to behold. Cautious at first, a little uncertain of this new environment, they wouldn't take long to realise the joys of liberation, taking off round the field in a mad gallop, bucking and leaping and kicking up their heels. Even the most old and staid of matrons would throw off their inhibitions and join in.

Calves were born, and usually gave birth without trouble, although some occasionally needed help too, sometimes mechanical help. A cow with a calf was to be avoided; they would defend their young ferociously, especially if a dog was about. Later, in my teen years, I was attacked by an irate cow (fortunately of the hornless Galloway breed) while my dad and I were moving her and her calf from one field to another. She shoved me along with her head until I fell on my back, when thankfully she came to a halt without trampling on me. But I'll never forget that angry, snorting black face glaring down at me.

Kittens were born, our pet mice and rabbits had babies. Animal reproduction held no mysteries for me, although I was hazy about the way they were created. When a bull was brought to visit one of our cows, I was kept inside, although my brother must have been allowed to watch the proceedings as he later attempted to enlighten me about the details, maybe not altogether accurately. I did not make the connection between animal and human reproduction for quite some time, however. The 'facts of life' were not a subject for family discussion in those days. At some point, mightily embarrassed, my mother gave me a leaflet to read. I declined and, equally embarrassed, told her I knew all that already. By then, from reading and from the school playground, I had learned the rudiments, though again not completely accurately. I read the agony aunt pages in my mum's and Auntie's women's magazines, but they were incredibly coy about plain speaking and I basically had to work things out for myself.

Spring was a magical time of year, with new life bursting out whichever way you looked. A haze of green would begin to appear on trees and bushes, gradually unfurling into stems and buds and leaves. The hawthorn tree beside our yard gate would be covered with sweet-smelling creamy flowers; the first bumble bees would crawl out of their winter homes underground and buzz sleepily about in the May blossom. When bluebells appeared, bowing their graceful heads in a haze of blue/mauve among the undergrowth, and one of us would triumphantly announce that we had heard the cuckoo for the first time that year, we would know that summer was just around the corner.

CHAPTER SEVENTEEN

Summer

Shall I compare thee to a summer's day?
Thou art more lovely and more temperate
Rough winds do shake the darling buds of May
And summer's lease hath all too short a date.

William Shakespeare

The summers of my childhood were long; they were hot, the sun shone and there was never a grey day. Or at least, that is how I remember them. The reality was probably very different. I loved summer, when we could be out of doors all day long, everything was green and the trees were in full leaf. I loved that if one stood, sat or lay under a tree, one looked up into a canopy of green, moving gently if there was a soft breeze, with splashes of sunlight dappling the undergrowth.

But summer on the farm was not a time for being idle, or at least not for the hard-working grown-ups. Early in summer would be shearing time, the flock having been 'washed' a few days before, which meant a quick dip in the washpool across the road, one at a time, in and out again. On shearing day, a mass of woolly bodies would be crammed into the big bay of the barn, bleating and bewildered as lambs and their mothers lost each other in the melee. My father would shear them one by one on the barn floor, bending his long back over a ewe immobilised into a sitting position against him and held there with one arm while with the other he plied the whirring shearing-head, stripping in long smooth strokes the wool that rolled off in a creamy wave of fleece. The fleece would be gathered up, and the pitch-pot called for to apply the owner's mark to the newly shorn animal; if a sheep had been accidentally nicked in the process, a dab of black oil would also be applied against infection. The sheep, strangely thin and naked, would be released to search among the bleating mass for her lamb, while my father straightened up and stretched his aching back for a moment before starting on the next.

Our job, when we were big enough, was to select a sheep from the milling press of bodies, catch it by its woolly coat and propel it to where my father, with a deft grab of a leg and flick of its body, would have the next candidate in position. Between the barn's big beams hung the woolsack, an enormous Hessian bag for receiving the fleeces. My mother and aunt rolled the fleeces. There was an art in folding a fleece; laid flat with the creamy underside on top, the untidy leg and neck bits tucked in, the whole thing rolled and tied with the hind leg pieces into a neat bundle. These went into the woolsack. When we were little we were sometimes put into the woolsack, where we fulfilled two purposes: we trod down the fleeces to pack them tight and make room for more, and we were safely out of harm's way. We swung gently or stood peering over the edge at the activity. When we were a little bigger, we'd be sat down at a safe distance with a pile of old copies of *Farmer and Stockbreeder*, which had a children's page in the back of the home section where we could follow the cartoon adventures of three piglet brothers called Peter, Paul and Percy, or do a puzzle or read a story. Ringing in our ears all day would be the sounds of the whirring machine, the bleating of disconsolate lambs separated from their mothers, the deeper voices of the ewes and the blissful reunions when they would find each other again. There were times of frustration when combs and cutters broke or clogged up, or a shower of rain meant a damp fleece, or the engine failed. Shearing was hard work, it was intensive and it was stressful.

Haymaking would be next, and that was hard work too, and not without its own stresses. I loved the hay meadows before they were cut, full of pink and white clover, delicate lady's smock, creamy meadowsweet, purple vetches and blue scabious. The grasses seemed very tall, taller than a small child's head, the ground beneath full of insect life and the buzzing of wild bees. My father anxiously listened to the weather forecast as grass ripened for mowing; a shower of rain on cut hay could make the difference between a good crop or a musty, unhealthy one. Good haymaking weather was hot sun and a gentle breeze, which would produce a sweet-smelling, dry crop full of nutrients for winter fodder. Wet hay, however much it was turned and aired, quickly lost its goodness and became heavy, mouldy, musty and liable to heat when stored, or could even burst into flames. So my father and others like him planned and fretted and worked like crazy when the weather was right.

Once the hay lay in green swathes across the field, it had to be worked upon, turned, tossed, turned again. I can't remember at which point mechanical turners came upon the scene, but I do recall turning hay by hand with wooden rakes. And my father using Captain to pull the horse-rake, with its high seat for the driver, which gathered the swathes of hay; at intervals a handle was pulled that released the hay and dropped it into manageable heaps for loading. Balers had not arrived when I was a small child; the hay was pitched up loose with a pikel into a high-ended wagon to be taken home. It was a treat – a somewhat perilous one, though the thought of danger never entered our heads – to be allowed to ride home on top of the swaying, creaking load. My dad would reach up his long arms and catch us as we slid to the ground. My mother would ride with us and he would catch her too; I have a memory of a tender moment or two between them as she slid into his arms.

Later in summer would come the corn harvest; again the standing ripe crops would be far above our heads, this time golden stalks topped with the nodding heads of oats, the stiff spikes of wheat or the whiskery piles of barley. No combine harvesters then. Out would come the binder, and round and round the field it would go, spitting out bound sheaves of corn upon a short stiff golden stubble, which gleamed brightly in the sun but scratched small bare legs painfully when walked upon. This time our job was to pick up the sheaves and set them in stooks – five or six sheaves to a stook – again, for ease of gathering, but also to ensure that the stems did not rot from contact with damp ground, and to allow air to flow through. All hands would be pressed into service; there was no time to go home for tea, so we would often have tea in the field, a great treat in our opinions. The little primus would be pumped up to boil the whistling kettle, bread and butter, cheese, cake and scones unpacked from the basket, and we would picnic in the shade of the hedge. Another happy memory of family togetherness is of walking home after a day in the fields, the sun dipping down and casting long shadows, us children running ahead of our parents. I glanced back at them and saw them silhouetted against the setting sun, walking together, holding hands and laughing. My world was secure.

A less pleasant side of harvesting was the panic of the rabbits and small mammals who would find themselves trapped in a shrinking patch of corn as the binder circumnavigated the field. There would come the point when they would burst from cover and make a frantic dash for safety. Rabbits were rightly considered a pest; the deadly myxamatosis that ended the threat from rabbits had not yet arrived, and there were far too many of them decimating growing crops. The aim was to kill as many as possible with sticks as they emerged from cover. The thrill of the hunt would possess the watchers as they leapt into action with loud rallying cries. Even we children were given sticks and pressed into service. From being friends and protectors of wildlife – in our own eyes at least – we had become their enemies and killers. I was reluctant. Just once, infected by bloodlust and hollering like a savage, I encountered a cowering rabbit and whacked it with my stick. I was immediately consumed with remorse and threw away my stick. I've never forgotten.

We kept a beehive in the corner of the garden, and sometime in late summer we would have a day or two of bee and honey work. Mostly the bees took care of themselves, but this required the help of Mr Fraporte, a Dutch bee expert who lived in a cottage, in the village near the bottom of the steep hill we had to take to get home, that was known as Cutter's Pitch. The name came from the man who had lived there previously, who had been a local livestock castrator. Mr Fraporte would arrive by bike and don his beekeeper uniform of white overalls tied tightly at the ankles to deter crawling bees, a large wide-brimmed hat covered by a veil, and strong gloves, and would go to work with his puffer, which doped the bees into a sleepy state and enabled easier extraction of the full honeycombs. A syrup substitute was given to the bees to replace the lost honey and to get them through the winter. Poor bees, they were hard-working creatures and had toiled all summer gathering pollen for their combs. No wonder they objected. Mr Fraporte never got stung, but the rest of us sometimes did.

There would then be a couple of days' activity indoors, spinning the honey extractor that removed the liquid honey by centrifugal force, to drain into the waiting honey pots. Odd bits of comb had to be filtered out. It was a sticky business, but not unpleasant, and the resultant pots of clear golden honey were very satisfying and delicious on bread and butter or in puddings.

Summer meant long, light evenings when we wanted to linger out of doors; it meant ripe strawberries in the garden and tiny wild ones on the banks; it meant fresh peas and beans and new potatoes, freedom from school and the occasional outing to the seaside, with a long bus ride, a day of sand and salt and sunburn, and fish and chips on the way home.

And then there were the summer visitors.

Relatives tended to visit more often during the summer months, mostly on Sunday afternoons, dressed up and ready for an inspection of the crops and the garden, followed by Sunday tea. It was mostly grown-up stuff and to be endured rather than enjoyed.

But we had visitors who really interested us and they were not relatives or neighbours. They were children. Boys, to be precise. I always preferred playing with boys at that stage of my childhood; maybe from necessity but also because they played much more exciting and adventurous games. Taken on a visit by one of my aunts to another of her relatives, I was sent to play with the younger daughter, a little younger than myself. I was totally bored by her games, and very relieved when her elder sister came along with a pony and saved the day. One summer visitor was Brian Lewis, who would stay during the holidays with his grandmother and his Aunt Joan at Tynessa, which perched overlooking some of our fields. Brian was my age and he, Ron and I quickly made friends and became almost inseparable during his visits. Brian was a fair-haired, good-looking lad, tall and athletic, who had a nice smile and walked with a spring in his step. We played cricket and rounders and had running races; he usually won but I could give him a good run for his money. Later Brian would become a professional athlete and run at the White City. He would also die of a heart attack at far too young an age. But none of this cast shadows on our holidays. The three of us would drift from our house to his and back again, talking, inventing games, requesting refreshments. We even visited the neighbours together, especially Alice Price at Bythel who could always be relied upon to supply freshly-baked bread or cakes or sweets.

The other summer visitors were the Fletchers, a family from Oldham who came for their summer holiday to stay at Crossway down the road, where Mrs Harris ran a B&B. They seemed very exotic to our eyes, with different accents, different views on the world and none of the natural reticence of country folk; especially the mother, Agnes, a large, florid-faced lady who talked a great deal and spoke her mind. Her husband, Norman, a quiet, kind, gentle man, seemed in her shadow but I felt they were a happy couple. The two boys, John and Albert, were, I think, eleven and nine when they first visited. John was a tall, curly-haired, confident boy; Albert, I think, had his mother's looks and his father's personality. I was seven and Ron was five, but the two of them kindly took us under their wings and we loved their visits. Town born and bred, John and Albert loved the countryside and couldn't get enough of it. We traipsed up hill and down dale with them, exploring the places we knew and seeing them afresh with their eyes. Together we dammed the stream at the bottom of our wood, lugging stones and carrying mud to fill the gaps. When we had a sizeable dam, we looked for craft to sail upon it. John showed us how to make rafts with sticks bound together; he was a Boy Scout back home and we were lost in admiration at the sturdy pocket-knife he had and the things he could do with it.

They came faithfully every year, and each time we fell back into our easy friendship and comradeship without a hitch – until the summer when John was sixteen, and suddenly he no longer wanted to play our games. He had grown several inches since the year before and sauntered about, hands in pockets, critically observing everything. He seemed almost a man. He was growing up, and the rest of us had been left behind.

We kept in touch with the Fletchers for many years. Sometimes Norman and Agnes would visit and reminisce over old times. John emigrated to South Africa and settled there. He and Albert both married; John had a family but Albert didn't. Agnes and I wrote for a while but finally we lost touch.

September would come, the swallows depart for warmer climes, the harvests would be gathered in, blackberries and hips and haws would be ripening in the hedgerows. A new school term would loom on the horizon. Summer would be over.

CHAPTER EIGHTEEN

Autumn

Autumn – the year's last, loveliest smile.

William Cullen Bryant

'Season of mists and mellow fruitfulness,' my mother would declaim when September came, quoting from *Ode to Autumn* by Keats. And it was so. Quite often, a new day would be heralded by a light mist rising from ground level, which burned off as the sun rose in the sky. The sun would be noticeably lower in the sky though, and the days beginning to pull in. But September was certainly a month of fruitfulness and plenty. The harvest would still be in the process of being gathered in, leaving fields of golden stubble, which all too soon would be adorned with a scattering of good old farmyard muck, and ploughed again for next year's crops. There would be a great ingathering also of ripened vegetables and fruits. Potatoes, swedes, carrots, parsnips would be dug and stored in the dark, onions pulled up and strung in long ropes to hang from the beams. Apples would be picked and carefully stored – any bruising would be a starting place for rot – plums turned into jam, excess vegetables pickled or used for chutney. We scoured the hedgerows for ripe brown hazelnuts, tumbling out of their shells, and cracked them between two stones. We picked luscious blackberries for pies and tarts and added to cooking apples for jam. Shiny brown horse-chestnuts spilled from spiky green cases, to be seized on with delight and collected for conker games at home and at school.

Autumn meant leaves changing colour, the smell of leaf-mould, and smoky bonfires burning garden debris. We would have a modest celebration at Hallowe'en, maybe just a hollowed-out swede or two carved into faces with candles inside, and an attempt at bobbing for apples. Sometimes we made toffee apples. November 5th saw an equally modest affair with a bonfire and a few fireworks; usually by then it was wet, cold and muddy out of doors. Autumn always meant mud, as the dry dust of the yard soaked up rain. There could be storms with strong winds rattling round the house and causing fresh draughts inside. If there was a lot of rain, the stream flowing down behind the buildings to the right sometimes diverted and poured down the yard outside our back door. A dry autumn was a joy, a wet one not so much.

Autumn was the time when our mother would exchange our cotton interlock underwear for warm woollens. We might have gone bare-legged most of the summer; now was the time for the thick woolly socks pulled up to the knees. Auntie might have knitted us some jumpers for the coming winter. Our shoes and wellies would be overhauled and repaired if possible; more likely our feet would have grown and we'd need to be measured for new sturdy winter boots. Ron's would be hobnailed; mine were more genteel, brown leather with turn-down tops. If we'd grown a lot, we'd need new winter coats.

And as ever, it was a time for hard work. There had to be a good supply of firewood for warmth over the winter, Sometimes a tree had to be felled to replenish our fuel stocks. I'm sure my dad must have done his share of tree-felling, but what I remember best is the women of the household doing the job. On a suitable day, Mum and Auntie, overalled and with children in tow, would arm themselves with axes, iron wedges and cross-cut saw, and sally forth to cut down a tree. Ash and oak make the best firewood. We'd go down the meadow to our stretch of woodland sloping down to the stream, select a tree, and ponder the direction it should fall. That decided, they'd set to work with an axe, cut out a notch, insert a wedge to ensure it fell as planned, and go to work with the cross-cut saw, one at each end. Some way through, more wedges would be hammered in. We'd watch all agog for the first indication that the tree was coming down. Standing well back, we'd hear the first creak, see the first shudder and watch in a mixture of awe and excitement as the tree swayed, creaked and went down with a crash and a shivering of twigs and branches. There was something both poignant and heartbreaking in the felling of a tree. I don't know whether I cried as a child; later in life I've sometimes shed tears at the demise of a woodland giant.

The tree must have been brought home by mechanical means; I don't have a memory of that. The branches must have been sawn off and turned into logs on the saw bench, a scary and dangerous contraption run by a belt from a tractor engine. The logs were manually passed through the wicked revolving blade with a high metallic whining sound when a log went through. There were no protective guards. Our mother issued dire warnings about the saw bench; she knew of people who had lost digits or even limbs through careless use of one. She liked to illustrate her warnings with personal stories; e.g. we must never eat cakes hot from the oven, she knew someone's little boy who'd eaten a hot cake and he died! I heeded her warnings well; even now, the ringing sound of a saw bench gives me an uneasy feeling. Likewise, the threshing drum. When the corn had been harvested, it would soon be threshing time. Trevor Harris would come with his threshing machine, which would be set up in our rickyard, and there'd be a hum of activity for a day or two. Neighbours would be there to help, one cutting the ties on the sheaves and feeding them into the machine, another on top pushing them into its churning innards, someone else working the chutes the corn came out of, two of them side by side; when one sack was full, that chute would be closed off and the other come into use, while the full sack was tied up and carried away up the granary steps, to be added to the growing sea of grain on the granary floor. Someone else would be dealing with the straw that spewed out at the other end, and there'd always be a terrier or two about on the lookout for escaping rats. The person on top of the drum had the most dangerous job, exposed to the busy machinery without a safety guard, or if there was a guard, it might well have been removed for convenience. People had been known to fall into the drum, my mother informed us darkly. My vivid imagination would go into overdrive and I couldn't wait to see the back of the thing.

Threshing was one of the times when a gang of neighbours had to be fed, coming in for tea, bread, cheese and cake at mid-morning 'bait', then for a full cooked dinner and pudding at one o'clock, and tea again when the afternoon ended. It seemed very strange to see our kitchen full of deep-voiced men sitting round the table, eating, drinking, talking laughing, some maybe smoking, joking, exchanging farming gossip, making a social occasion of it. I was fascinated but shy, and dreaded that one of them would speak to me and require a reply. Mostly I kept out of the way.

The fox-hunting season would begin in early November, and it was a common thing to hear the baying of hounds, rallying to the call of the hunting horn, and see a group of red-coated riders galloping across the fields in pursuit of some hapless fox. My father grumbled sometimes about the cutting up of the ground from the galloping hooves. My sympathies were mostly with the fox, but all the same there was something rather thrilling about the spectacle. I made up my mind that if I ever encountered a fleeing fox, I would hide it in one of our buildings and thwart those hounds. I'd been told that foxhounds could be savage beasts; there was a tale about a huntsman who'd gone to feed his hounds, fallen over, and nothing had been found of him except his boots.

Autumn was also the time for pig-killing, a nasty business from beginning to end. When I was older I would run as far away as I could across the fields and stay away as long as possible, although there was no way of avoiding it. Whether the pig knew of his impending fate or whether he just resented being manhandled, I don't know, but he would set up a shrill, terrified screaming at the first touch of the hands that had come to take him to the slaughter. This took place on the barn floor, swept clean for the purpose, with the pig-killing bench set up in readiness. Our local pig-killer was Alwyn Jones. I never saw it done, but it cannot have been pleasant, nor had humane slaughter methods yet been implemented. There must have been terror, and blood, and pain. Later I would see the pig's corpse, disembowelled and hung from a hook in the barn rafters, and there would be the smell of singeing hair and flesh as the bristles were burnt off for easier management of the butchering. Our neighbour Tom Lloyd would visit next day to help with the cutting up of the carcase, when our pet pig would be reduced to cuts of meat, ribs, hams, shoulders, somehow less terrifying than that complete carcase. A disgusting and evil-smelling part of pig killing was the bathtub of guts and entrails that would be brought into the house, purple-blue, slimy and steaming. Several of us would crouch round the bathtub, where the task was to strip the fat from the innards; later it would be rendered down for lard. It was a revolting task, especially when someone careless and heavy-handed happened to rupture a part of the intestine. My mother would boil the head and strip the flesh from it to make brawn, the trotters could be pickled, the bladder inflated and used as a football, though I'm not sure we ever did that. The only thing going to waste from the killing of a pig was the squeak (the windpipe), I was told.

I hated the whole messy, miserable business; it was worse even than the Christmas feathering. However, as at Christmas, I recovered to enjoy the liver and the scratchings (odd bits of meat, mainly fat) fried up until crisp and brown, and the roast ribs of pork when they came around. Brown paper parcels of meat would be taken round to the neighbours, who would return the favour when their own pig was killed. And by the time winter came and we had crisp fried bacon and eggs, or succulent ham, or bacon boiled with cabbage, my scruples would be quite forgotten.

CHAPTER NINETEEN

Winter

When icicles hang by the wall
And Dick the shepherd blows his nail
And Tom bears logs into the hall
And milk comes frozen home in pail
When blood is nipped and ways be foul
Then nightly sings the staring owl, to-whoo;
To – whit, to-whoo, a merry note
While greasy Joan doth keel the pot.

William Shakespeare

Winter meant grey days, wet days, dull days, short days, Wellington boots and mud. Winter days began late and ended early, and the nights were long. Christmas was a bright spot in the midst of it all, and then we settled to the real business of winter.

Real winter began in January, when the days were just almost imperceptibly beginning to grow longer. 'As the days lengthen, the cold strengthens' was a saying I heard often, and it was true. If there was snow (and without exception there was, back then), it would come in January, maybe drifting lazily down in big soft flakes, or, causing more concern, small fine particles driven by a fierce wind which blew snow into drifts and found a way into every nook and cranny and crevice. There might have been the odd flurry in December or even November, but I don't remember many white Christmases. The snow would come, and our hearts would rejoice. No question of school for a while. Instead, a silent world blanketed in white beckoned. We never gave a thought to frozen water supplies, sheep and cattle having to be foddered and littered, deep snow and treacherous ice to be negotiated while carrying hay, straw, water and milk buckets, firewood, coal, all in freezing temperatures and sometimes blizzard conditions. We couldn't wait to get out into that magic muffled whiteness, find a steep smooth place for sledging (we were given a brand-new sledge one memorable Christmas), build igloos, make

107

a snowman, throw snowballs at each other and at other targets. We broke off icicles that formed around the corrugated roof of the back porch and sucked on them. We tracked the marks of birds and animals in the snow, looked them up in our nature books and recorded what we'd seen. We rolled about in drifts; there'd be rows of wet woolly gloves, scarves and hats drying and steaming on the fireguard. We added to the wet puddles on the floor which formed on the flagstones from the boots of whoever had been outside. Everyone, adult and child, would wear extra layers of clothing. My father, like most farmers, would drape a Hessian sack around his shoulders for extra protection in extreme weather. There'd be extra blankets on our beds, and we needed them.

We didn't mind the bitterly cold spells; we dug in, hunkered down and stuck it out. And when the thaw came, with a softening and shrinking of the snow, a tinkling and dripping and running of water, and bare patches of earth beginning to appear, brown and muddy green, we children were quite sorry. Contact with the outside world would be resumed, the postman would be able to make his rounds again, and one day we'd greet with long faces the news that Mr Powell's school transport would be running again on Monday.

Winter evenings were cosy, with the outside work done early, the cold and dark shut out and all of us gathered round the fire and the lamplit kitchen table. Nobody went off into another room to do their own thing; it would have been far too cold anyway, and we all wanted to be a part of that circle of light and warmth. There were various activities that were often joint efforts. We all shared in the making of rag rugs, using old clothing cut into strips and hooked through a background of sacking. Those Hessian sacks had many uses apart from the intended one. It was possible to get quite creative with colours and patterns and designs. I think even my father joined in the rug-making occasionally. Afterwards the rugs were backed with more Hessian to conceal the underside, and we'd have a new rug for the kitchen or to go beside a bed. Very comforting for bare toes on a chilly morning. Another evening activity was the making of spills from tightly rolled old newspaper, for lighting candles and lamps from the fire to save on matches. A pot of spills stood ready on the mantelpiece along with the tea-caddy and other assorted useful and decorative items. One of these was a brown and white pottery dog which I think belonged to my aunt, and which I have inherited.

We read, we listened to the wireless, we knitted, sewed, wrote, drew, made models. We played card and board games, did word games and quizzes. It did not occur to us to be bored.

Some winters were especially hard, and in particular the winter of 1947 when I was six years old. That winter was later recorded as Britain's coldest and hardest for two hundred years. It had started mild, but heavy snow came in mid-January and brought several subsequent spells of severe cold and blizzard conditions that lasted until March. My only clear memory of that time is standing at our back door and seeing banks of snow towering far above my head on either side of the tunnel my dad had dug to let us out.

Post-war Britain was ill-prepared for such a harsh winter and was hard hit. Roads and railways were at a standstill; power stations, unable to access fuel, were forced to close down, cutting off electricity supplies to businesses, hospitals, schools and private homes. Schools were closed, no great hardship to the children of Britain, but so were many shops, which was a great hardship. There were food shortages; vegetables frozen in the ground, half of the sheep in Wales dying. In some parts, five feet of snow covered the ground, with drifts of up to twenty feet. Hedges disappeared under drifting snow, becoming level with the roads and lanes, even the telegraph poles. The situation was so grave that at one time the American Air Force stationed in Britain was deployed to parts of the Welsh countryside, where they dropped fodder for starving animals cut off by the snow. Nevertheless, many cattle and sheep, whole herds and flocks, starved or froze to death. Birds fell frozen from their perches; there were reports of hundreds of dead rabbits found around a snow-covered hayrick, unable to reach the food.

And there were human tragedies, even one very close to us. Our neighbour Dickie just up the hill and a hundred yards or so from our road gate, an elderly man living alone, slipped on ice outside his cottage, was unable to get up and froze to death. A sledge had to be brought to remove the body when it was discovered.

Living on a more or less self-sufficient farm, we were better off than many of the populations of towns and cities. We had food, we had firewood, we were independent of gas and electricity, although I don't know what we did if the oil or paraffin ran out. We piled coats on the bed if we were still cold – and going to bed was a chilly experience in an unheated room. By morning there would be frost patterns on the inside of the window, and if there was washing water in the basin it would be topped by a sheet of ice. It must have been gruelling work caring for the livestock in those conditions, but I don't think we had any great losses. We survived. What we couldn't get, we substituted; what we couldn't substitute, we did without. We made do. We managed.

Making do and managing was one of my mother's great strengths, partly, I suppose, because she'd been the youngest of a large family, but maybe mainly because of the shortages of the war years. I think she was also naturally frugal; nothing in our house was ever wasted. Leftover food would be recycled in some way, or if not, there were cats and a dog and pig waiting to be fed. She made dresses from old curtains, pillowslips from old dresses, tea-towels and dishcloths from old pillowslips. The tea towels ended their days as floor-cloths. She saved everything, from bits of elastic to make garters for our socks, to buttons and hooks and eyes from old defunct garments, even the metal fastenings from old stretched-out suspenders. She hoarded ends of soap in a jar with the intention of making a new bar of soap – it usually ended up as a horrible sludge. Candles were something we usually had a good supply of, but my mother saved candle wax, just in case. I'm not sure whether she ever attempted candle-making, but it wouldn't surprise me. She unravelled old jumpers with holes in the elbows to knit up into children's jerseys and pullovers. She patched my father's overalls until there were patches on patches. The Welsh wool socks she knitted took many years to wear out, but when they did, she darned them.

The winter of 1947 came to an end with a parting shot of the heaviest snowfall of the winter over Scotland on March 1st. This seems to have been the harsh weather's last fling. Very soon temperatures were rising across the country and a thaw setting in. This happened quickly and, along with heavy rain and strong winds, created serious flooding as the snow-melt poured off the frozen ground into the rivers. The winter had ended as dramatically as it had begun.

Most of our winters came to an end more gently, with the traditional rain in February, strong cold winds in March giving way to the softer feeling in the air in April, though that month could sometimes be a treacherous one too. When lambs appeared in the fields, later born than they are today, and we saw the first swallow coming home to nest after its long journey from warmer climes, we knew that we'd seen the last of winter for another year.

CHAPTER TWENTY

A Year of Change

Times change, and we with time...

Anon.

Nineteen fifty-two was a year of change, nationally, internationally and within our family. King George VI died on February 6th and was succeeded by his twenty-five-year-old daughter Elizabeth, our present Queen. I remember that morning at school when Miss Anthony did an unheard-of thing: she left her class of infants unattended and came into the Top Class, where we heard her telling Mr Evans in hushed tones, 'I've just heard on the wireless that the King has passed away!'

Suddenly the face of the new young Queen was in every newspaper and magazine, tracing her ancestry, her life from babyhood, her 1947 wedding and her two adorable small children. The new Elizabethan age had begun.

A few weeks after the King's death, on February 26th, Winston Churchill announced that Britain now had the atomic bomb. An atomic explosion in Nevada followed in April, and in November came the first detonation of a thermonuclear weapon over an island in the Pacific Ocean. War was rumbling in Korea, while Kenya saw the beginning of the Mau-Mau uprising. In March, tornadoes raged across the southern United States, killing three hundred and forty-three people. Agatha Christie's long-running play *The Mousetrap* opened in London in October and has never closed. The first frozen peas were sold in shops. From December 5th to December 9th, a blanket of fog covered London, so dense that traffic could not run safely; there were deaths among children, the elderly, and those with bronchial problems; hospitals were packed and stretched to their limits. It was discovered that smoke from coal fires combined with the thick fog made the lethal mixture they named 'smog' and led eventually to the installation of the Clean Air act later in the decade.

Nearer home, a life ended and a life began. Our grandmother died and my brother was born, within the space of a few weeks that summer. I remember the night my granny died. For some time, she had been bedridden, not the same granny who had tucked us up in bed when our mum was busy, or who pottered in the house and garden, or greeted us with a hug when we returned from school. She lay in bed, small and pale and frail, and we had been told that she would not be getting better. A succession of family members had been to visit in the months before her death.

That night she was delirious, talking a babble of unintelligible words that I could hear from the next bedroom, the one that had to be passed through to get to hers. Half-asleep, I was aware of the to-ing and fro-ing of my mother and my aunt, talking in hushed voices. Even my father passed through at one point, an occurrence that to my knowledge had never happened before. There were dim lights, and whispered conversations that went on until I fell asleep. In the morning I was awakened early by Auntie, who asked me to go into my parents' bedroom with my brother until it was time to get up. She told me it was because Mrs Williams, Birds Nest would shortly be arriving to attend to Granny. Mrs Williams was the local unofficial midwife, nurse and layer-out of the deceased. I knew in my heart that Granny had died, but I tried to convince myself that Mrs Williams was just coming to help with the nursing, so I asked how Granny was. I don't know whether I cried or not at the news that she had died; by the time my brother woke, I was feeling a strange relief that her sufferings were over, and I philosophically told him that I thought her death was a good thing. Ron did not agree, and was indignant and tearful. That same morning, Auntie Mary came and whisked us away to stay for a few days.

We did not attend the funeral. My mother, ever protective, must have decided that it would be too sad and distressing for us. Afterwards, neighbours visited. Joan Millward, the young woman from Tynessa, had lost her mother just the year before, a few weeks before she gave birth to her son Haydn. She warned my mother that the shock and grief of bereavement could lead to a premature birth.

However, my mother went the distance and gave birth to my brother at the appointed time. It was an early July day and it was hot, hot, hot. Sometime in the morning, Ron and I were given a huge pile of comics, donated by Joan Millward and her nephew Brian, and carefully hoarded by my mother against this occasion. It was a brilliant idea. A pile of unread comics, full of undiscovered treasure, ready to be discovered and nothing to do but read them! We thought we were in heaven. For hours we sat and lay in the shade of the buddleia bush by the wall in a corner of the garden, with bees buzzing and butterflies flitting among the sweet-smelling purple blooms. We almost forgot the important events unfolding indoors as we perused the adventures of *Stainless Stan the Iron Man*, *Morgyn the Mighty*, *Limp-along Leslie*, *Genghis Khan and his Mongol Hordes* and countless others. No matter that they were boys' comics and mostly in text and not picture-strips, those were the ones I loved, with their drama and action and excitement. What happened for lunch I don't remember, but sometime in the afternoon there was a flurry of activity from the house. The midwife must have been there for some time, but labour had not progressed as quickly as it should, and she had decided the doctor must be called. My father had been dispatched to the phone box maybe half a mile away at the crossroads near Plaswarren, to make the call. However, things speeded up after he'd gone, the doctor was not needed after all, so Ron was sent off after our dad to intercept the call.

After a while we were ushered in to meet our new brother, a healthy seven and a half pounds and looking, at first impression, like a little pink frog with a tuft of dark hair. He was dressed in a big terry nappy, a vest and, of all things, a pink matinee jacket. I think Mum and Auntie had hedged their bets by preparing equal amounts of pink and blue baby clothes; no inkling of the gender of a baby *in utero* in those days. So we had blue and we had pink, and of course we must not waste anything by not using them, though why they had chosen pink for his first day of life is beyond me. Or why a knitted matinee jacket on a boiling summer day, although of course my mother was a firm believer in wrapping up warm.

His names had long been decided; for months it was to be Diana for a girl, Timothy for a boy. So Timothy Robert he became, Timmy for short.

Timmy must have been a good baby, for I have little memory of him crying. Maybe he had no reason to cry for long; everyone in the family doted on him and took every opportunity to pick him up and cuddle him. I do remember rocking him to sleep in his pram, back and fore, back and fore, gradually lessening the motion in the hope he wouldn't notice and I'd be able to go off about my own devices. It never worked; the moment the rocking tailed off and stopped, his eyes would fly open and be followed by an indignant wail.

I took the eleven-plus that year, passed highest in the school and was headed for the County Grammar School in Llandrindod Wells. This meant the purchase of a whole new uniform in navy and yellow. My cousin Margaret had attended the school some years before, and Auntie Mary helpfully donated some of the necessary clothing items, notably a gymslip and a hat. I had a brand-new blazer, emblazoned with the school motto – *Surge Age* ('Be up and doing'), a gabardine raincoat, white blouses, a yellow and navy striped tie, navy shorts and gym shirt and plimsolls, a satchel and P.E. bag. The second-hand items proved to be a source of mortification when I started school in September; the other girls' gymslips were brand new and had crisp, sharp box pleats. The pleats in mine had been ironed many times and had a tired look, and the back was slightly shiny from much sitting. The hat, a beret style with the school motto on the front, had to be worn at all times outdoors; we were allowed into town at lunchtime but woe betide any student who sallied forth bare-headed. The other girls' hats had a lining of a pearly-grey colour, Margaret's had obviously worn through and Auntie Mary had replaced it with a blue lining. When someone commented and asked why mine was different, I feebly lied and said that was how it had come from the shop.

The first term went well, but things changed and problems developed. I was a painfully shy, sensitive child, the school journey was a killer, up at 6am and not home until 7, having walked the two and a half miles to and from where the bus put me off in Clyro. It would have helped enormously if the bus route had been my way, but it took the other road to Painscastle. And then there was homework to be done every evening. We tried lodging with Auntie Mary in the week, nearer to the bus route and nearer to school, but that did not work out either. I was horribly homesick all week and my work suffered, my test results steadily falling. I was offered lodgings in Llandrindod; some of the girls did that but I was devastated at the thought and refused to consider it. There were a few difficult months when I was deeply unhappy for the first time in my life.

Eventually, in desperation, my parents decided to change my school and I was transferred to Clyro Court Secondary Modern, now known as Baskerville Hall, a wonderfully gracious building set in beautiful grounds, where a grammar school education was lost to me but where my equilibrium was restored and, I believe, I was saved from a serious breakdown. I adored the new school, made good friends, some of whom remain to this day, and liked the easy ambience of the school, which was something of an experiment in education with an agricultural emphasis.

I did not realise it at the time, but slowly, gradually, almost imperceptibly I was beginning to leave behind the blue remembered hills of childhood and start on the challenging, scary, nerve-wracking and exciting adventure of growing up.

Contact the Author

To contact the author, please write to:

Eleanor Watkins
c/o Onwards and Upwards Publishers
4 The Old Smithy
London Road
Exeter
EX5 2EA

Or send an email to:

eleanorw18@hotmail. com

Or visit the author's Facebook page for more information:

www.facebook.com/eleanorwatkinsbooks

What Shall I Read Next?

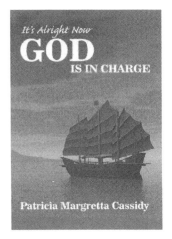

It's Alright Now – God is in Charge
Patricia Margretta Cassidy
ISBN 978-1-907509-84-1

The Second World War and the events that followed shaped Patricia's life as her missionary family travelled from country to country and across three continents. From tigers and bandits to submarines and war camps, the stories of her family highlight the risks, dangers and sufferings experienced in Asia and Africa during that important historical period. Yet we also see how faith in Jesus can guide a family through every trial.

Vicky's Journey from East to West
Vicky Meyer
ISBN 978-1-78815-635-6

Vicky Meyer (a.k.a. Grace Ann Chalkley) spent her early childhood in China, during which time the Japanese Army invaded Pearl Harbour, and foreigners in China were now considered enemies of Japan. As a result, Vicky's school were first required to remain in the school compound, and then later taken to the same concentration camp as Olympic athlete Eric Liddell.

Books available from all good bookshops
and from the publisher:

www.onwardsandupwards.org